CRICKET
CHARACTERS

THE CRICKETER CARICATURES OF JOHN IRELAND
TEXT BY CHRISTOPHER MARTIN-JENKINS

STANLEY PAUL
LONDON · MELBOURNE · AUCKLAND · JOHANNESBURG

Stanley Paul & Co. Ltd

An imprint of Century Hutchinson Ltd
62-65 Chandos Place, London WC2N 4NW
Century Hutchinson (Australia) Pty Ltd
16-22 Church Street, Hawthorn, Melbourne, Victoria 3122
Century Hutchinson (NZ) Ltd
32-34 View Road, Glenfield, Auckland 10
Century Hutchinson (SA) Pty Ltd
PO Box 337, Bergvlei 2012, South Africa

First published 1987
Copyright © Lennard Books 1987

Made by Lennard Books Ltd
Mackerye End, Harpenden, Herts AL5 5DR

Editor Michael Leitch
Designed by Pocknell & Co
Production Reynolds Clark Associates Ltd

British Library Cataloguing in Publication Data

Martin-Jenkins, Christopher
Cricket characters,
1. Cricket players — Portraits
I. Title II. Ireland, John
796.35'8'0922   GV915.A1

ISBN 0 09 172626 3

Printed and bound in Italy by Motta, Milan

CONTENTS

INTRODUCTION

I T IS SOMETIMES SAID, although without exception it is old timers who say it, that there are no characters left in cricket. It is nonsense, of course. What has changed is the way that characters are presented to the public.

Television, especially, has brought cricketing heroes into people's homes. Every smile, every spit, every gesture, handsome or mean, is viewed by millions. Not only is there no privacy for the heroes of the game, there is also less opportunity for those who write about them to use their imagination.

No writer has had a richer imagination than Neville Cardus. Unfortunately there have been those who have questioned his standing as a writer by analysing some of his most outrageous stories and proving that they could never have happened. He certainly put words into the mouths of the cricketing giants of his day, but never maliciously so. Cardus reasoned, no doubt, that if they didn't say it, they should have done. I doubt, for example, that Wilfred Rhodes and Emmott Robinson really did have this exact conversation when they inspected a damp pitch one morning at Headingley:

'Reckon it'll be turning by two o'clock, Wilfred.'

'Nay, Emmott, half past . . .'

The point of relating this imaginary chat between two wily old pros was to illustrate the depth of thought they applied to the county game of their day.

I remember John Arlott once telling me an even more unlikely story of a game of bridge he was playing with Walter Hammond before a match at Gloucester one day. The rubber was interrupted by the tiresome need for Hammond to go out to bat. He proceeded to make a double hundred, returned in a pool of perspiration four hours later, and throwing his gloves into his bag as he re-entered the dressing-room, said simply: 'Four no trumps.'

What does it matter that imagination has embroidered the tale? Hammond was a heroic Adonis with many personal failings unknown to the public. The popular Press and television would probably have destroyed him had he been a contemporary player.

The game's Golden Age had no chronicler in the class of Cardus, or that other great sketcher of characters, Robertson-Glasgow. But it did have an artist called Leslie Ward, or 'Spy', who conveyed by skilled caricatures the character of many of the great names of his era. John Ireland's collection in this book is surely the finest collection of cricketing caricatures since Spy's.

The criterion for inclusion was necessarily somewhat haphazard and there are bound to be others whom followers of the game would have preferred to see between these covers than some of those who have been chosen. I would submit, in fact, that no man attains the higher reaches of cricket without having 'character', which can mean anything from being a stand-up comic to a gritty fighter who barely utters a word. I have greatly enjoyed organizing my thoughts on the 40 selected characters who have enlivened recent years of cricket watching; I have enjoyed even more the brilliant portrayals of John Ireland. They are destined, I think, to become collectors' treasures.

The only people who may *not* appreciate these drawings are the characters themselves. I certainly disown completely this ludicrous depiction!

THE BATSMEN

PERHAPS ONLY TWO PLAYERS, the Jamaicans George Headley and Lawrence Rowe, have made such an extraordinary entry into Test cricket as the one made by Azharuddin against England a few winters ago. Looking like a boy, with wrists no bigger than a fat man's fingers, he first made a painstaking hundred at Calcutta, an innings in context with the funereal pace of the match; then more brilliant centuries at Madras and Kanpur. He used those pencil-slim wrists as Ranji must once have done to glide, steer, glance and cut the ball to all corners of the ground.

A wonderful eye and calm temperament enabled him to take to Test cricket like a cuckoo to a nest. Inevitably much of what followed was an anti-climax but he is still destined to make a huge volume of runs, and no doubt a fortune, in the years ahead. He will charm millions of spectators on the way and drive countless bowlers to distraction.

He is unusual in the Indian side in that, as his first name suggests, he is a Moslem. His father is a clerk in the Government Electricity Department in Hyderabad. 'Azhar' himself was still wet behind the ears when his sudden fame arrived. He became the proud possessor of a motor-scooter, the first of many

riches to come his way. He had not yet discovered girls. Now, the romance of travel and the trappings of the good life are all that threaten his prospects as a batsman.

There seems little serious danger, however, that success will go to his head. He attributes all that has happened to him so far to the will of Allah and he smilingly but sheepishly accepts the plaudits which have come his way, a modest inspection of his feet being his answer to all congratulations.

In England in 1986 he was just a little disappointing, getting out while well set at Headingley when distracted by the crowd, an irony for a young man who had been untroubled by the noisy scrutiny of 80,000 in his first Test in Calcutta. He ended the tour, however, with 596 runs from 10 innings and next time, no doubt, he will put his experience to good effect.

The range of his strokeplay is already developing. He clips anything near leg stump to any part of the legside boundary, a sure sign of class, and off the back foot he seems to have time to choose whether to hit the ball past cover or mid-wicket. He has been known to steer off-spinners against the break past slip with moment-perfect timing. Genius is in his veins.

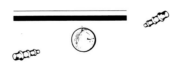

MOHAMMED AZHARUDDIN

IT SAYS A GOOD DEAL for the doggedness of Allan Border that he has batted at least as effectively, possibly even more so, since taking over the captaincy of an Australian team which, during the time of his leadership, has never been able to select from a full complement of players. Deprived of some hardened, and also some promising, cricketers who have been employed in South Africa, he has presided over a succession of disappointing performances and when the captain has been out their opponents as well as their supporters have often felt: 'The game's half over now.'

On many another occasion, however, he has staved off defeat with his own resolutely wielded bat. And let us not forget, either, that he has had his moments of triumph: a victory over the West Indies at Sydney; others there against New Zealand and England; and one over England at Lord's. Nor has it been all gloom in those many One-Day Internationals, of which Border has played more than anyone in the world. But it has generally been a big struggle and, in the process, much of the joy has gone out of his cricket.

He was always, it is true, a gritty little battler, with a fondness for a good scrap. You can see by his walk to the wicket, like a terrier out for a walk in a neighbourhood bristling with bigger dogs, that he is ready for a fight and not afraid of his ability to look after himself. He had to get used to battling against the odds pretty quickly for, in only his second Test, Australia folded cheaply twice against England and lost heavily. Border made 60 not out and 45 not out, but England won the Ashes.

He is a good fellow to have in a dressing-room, as well as in the middle: not a wag or a brilliant wit, but a solid citizen; the sort who encourages others just by being there. But leadership has not come naturally to him. It has made him a sterner, more anxious character than the brilliant, carefree player of his early days, who liked nothing better than to twinkle down the pitch to a spin bowler and loft him straight back over his head with a decisive, staccato thrust from strong forearms. Like all very fine players he waits until the last·moment before he commits himself to a stroke and his feet and head seem always to be in the right position. He had some early losing battles against the West Indian fast bowlers, but he later became one of the very few to enjoy a really successful series against them in the Caribbean. Against Joel Garner, in his most successful series, Malcolm Marshall, Michael Holding and either Wayne Daniel or Eldine Baptiste, chunky little left-handed Border scored 521 runs in 10 innings at an average of 74.

Brilliance and courage had been equally evident during his most remarkable single innings: his 123 not out in the second innings at Old Trafford in 1981. He batted throughout with a broken finger and it took him over six hours to score a hundred, every stroke he played giving him pain. This was the same man who as captain in England four years later began the tour with four hundreds in a row and ended it with eight in all. He may be past his peak when he again gets the chance to play in a strong Australian side but, if he can last the pace and keep up his appetite for runs, he is bound to retire as one of the heaviest scorers in all Test cricket.

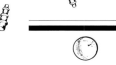

ALLAN BORDER

GEOFFREY BOYCOTT, the great but haunted batsman, was like one of those dogs bought on Christmas Eve from Battersea Dogs' Home. As if he had been maltreated as a puppy, he wanted desperately to be loved, but trusted no-one until he got to know them really well, often reacted irrationally even to those who meant him well, and never got over the feeling that the whole world was against him.

He built a fortress around himself, in life as at the wicket. The house that he eventually had built with some of his hard-earned riches was like a fortress too, keeping out those – above all the mischievous, hounding journalists – whose interest in him he could not accept as being a consequence of his prodigious achievements and his manner of attaining them.

What a batsman he was, though! Or perhaps I should have said, what a batsman he might have been! In a famous Gillette Cup Final at Lord's he won the match for Yorkshire single-handed, dominating a hapless Sussex attack like a rampant Visigoth cutting a swathe through a defenceless village. He hit three sixes and 15 fours in his 146 that afternoon, yet it was a wholly untypical performance for, like the orphan dog, his usual motto was 'safety first at all times'.

His technique was equalled in his time for watertight solidity only by Sunil Gavaskar: but he was less inclined to occasional flights of fancy than Gavaskar, and even harder to dig out. Because he believed that everyone was out to get him – personally – he was at his very best when things were tough. He faced the fastest and fiercest bowlers without a sign of a flinch, though in his early days his use of spectacles, and his later use of contact lenses, suggested imperfect eyesight. When he opted out of playing for England for a few years, an interregnum without which his record pile of runs for England would have been even larger, some mean and unknowledgable souls accused him of being battle-shy. Such voices were raised loudest in Australia. In the Yorkshire dressing-room they knew all about Geoffrey's faults, but they never accused him of running away once he got to the wicket.

In fact he was not to know that, in 1974–75, Dennis Lillee was about to relaunch a career apparently spoiled by serious injury, or that one Jeff Thomson was about to become much more than a name on Sheffield Shield scorecards. Years later, when Boycott began to give some stick to Lillee in Australia, a dauntless Yorkshire journalist turned to his counterpart in the Melbourne Press-box and said, blandly: 'I wonder why Lillee has been avoiding him all these years.'

No-one can ever have practised harder than Geoffrey. He would have a net anywhere at any time if only he could find bowlers. In the field, after looking slow and ragged as a young man, he soon forced himself to become accomplished. Off it he was frugal, watching his diet carefully, looking after himself at all times, guarding his priorities.

Geoffrey Boycott was a lonely perfectionist, unloved but grudgingly admired by those who knew him; adored by thousands who did not.

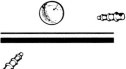

GEOFFREY BOYCOTT

MARTIN CROWE SAYS that his favourite player (following his boyhood hero, Gary Sobers) was Greg Chappell. He admired Chappell because he had a 'classic array of shots surrounding a solid, straight defence'. It is not a bad way to live your life to follow the example of someone you believe in and, a few years after he wrote these words, Crowe has followed Chappell, Australia's highest Test scorer, so faithfully that the description would apply neatly to his own batting style. Moreover it is as certain as anything in life can be that he himself will become New Zealand's highest Test scorer.

Before very long he is sure to follow his elder brother Jeff as captain of New Zealand. Martin was the first of the two to play Test cricket but this was mainly because Jeff had launched his own career in South Australia. They were impressed by him in Adelaide, enough to want him to move to Australia permanently and Jeff has turned out, having returned home, to be a reliable contributor in the middle-order, good enough to have got a Test hundred against the West Indies in the lions' den. But he would be the first to accept that his younger brother is out of an even higher drawer, one that most men never reach.

Martin Crowe is one of only a very few players who instantly strikes the knowledgeable watcher as something special. That God-given gift of time to play the ball has been used already to best advantage. So many players with a trace of genius use their talents carelessly, but Martin, with a mature approach and guidance and encouragement from his father, David, who himself played first-class cicket and who is young enough to be a friend to his boys, has dedicated himself to the ideal of a professional sportsman. At the age of 24 he had already scored seven Test hundreds, as many as Glenn Turner and Bev Congdon and more than any other New Zealander.

There is an enviable purity about all his cricket. He always looks immaculate, from his curly head to his clean boots. He is ideally built for a mixture of speed and hard work, being tall and strong but not too heavy. As a bowler he can be surprisingly quick and distinctly useful against any but the best: in a season in Yorkshire league cricket he was very successful with the ball as well as the bat. His batting itself is simply a model: never a graceless movement, never, it seems, a careless shot; head always over the ball, feet in the right position; looking always to get on top of the bowling, yet prepared to bide his time when conditions are hard.

He made such an impact when first he spent a year with Somerset that club officials were prepared to risk civil war by inviting him back at the expense of Richards and Garner, two of the greatest names in world cricket. He soon repaid them, coming back to Taunton by the earliest possible flight after New Zealand's tour of Sri Lanka had been aborted because of violence in Colombo. His commitment to his county was as great as it had been three years before when he had, of his own initiative, formed a club for the 2nd XI players to put more of a sense of purpose and direction into their cricket careers.

Already he has proved himself a natural cricketer and a natural leader of men. The seeds of greatness are in him and he is taking the greatest care to see that they will blossom and flourish.

MARTIN CROWE

WITH THAT CRINKLED, applejohn face, Keith Fletcher looks a bit like a jockey. When he was in charge of Essex, for year after year of success, the analogy was apt enough for he controlled the moves of his team with all the attributes of a skillful race-rider; a loose rein off the field, a tight one on it; a breather here, a call for all-out effort there; sometimes a waiting race, sometimes a dash from the stalls.

He has been the best modern county captain, with the possible exception of Mike Brearley, and it was one of cricket's great recent injustices that he should have been given so little time to show what he could do as a Test leader. Previous captains of England had always recognized and made use of his ability to sense the right tactics on the field, to plan a strategy off it, and to spot the weak points of opposition players. For Essex he has been adept at all these things and fearless in attacking the batsmen with a varied attack when his side were in the field. He handed on the captaincy to Graham Gooch in 1986 after leading them to a mantelpiece full of trophies, but he remained to advise and stand in for Gooch when he was asked to do so. Few would have handed on their job so willingly after such success and fewer still would have been prepared to stay on as number two.

Pale, rather frail-looking lad though he was, the 'Gnome' was something of a schoolboy prodigy. He looked apologetic as he walked to the crease, especially, it seemed, on the big occasion, but he used the bat with a marvellous instinctive skill, flicking the ball off his legs or thrashing it through the covers with perfect timing. 'Class, man, class,' purred a West Indian wicket-keeper after standing behind him for a few hours on his only visit to the Caribbean.

He went on all England's tours for many years, never tapping a consistent vein of runs but always contributing something useful. He tended to do better in the second innings than in the first, suggesting that he was rather too diffident for his own good and that it took him time to settle. He never seemed to relish very quick bowling, especially after the 1974–75 bombardment by Lillee and Thomson which left no England batsman unscarred, mentally if not physically. But he had plenty of success against bowling of all types and he was especially brilliant against spin, playing the ball very late with neat, watchful strokes.

He was for a long time rather wary of the Press, whom he referred to collectively as 'the spies', but he is really a warm and sociable character who enjoys a party and whose winter hobby is shooting. His accent is unmistakably East Anglian, exaggerated by a distinctive failure to pronounce his 'r's, which makes the nomenclature of his two daughters, Sara and Tamara, to whom he frequently refers with pride, somewhat unfortunate.

He has proved a special wizard at the one-day game, both as captain and as a batsman never shy to resort to the unorthodox. Spectators have often failed to realize how canny a player he is, especially in Yorkshire where it took them years to forgive him for being preferred in a Headingley Test to their own Phil Sharpe, only for him to spill several catches which Sharpe, a brilliant slip but a lesser batsman, would surely have gobbled. But professionals have never underestimated Keith Fletcher, the cricketers' cricketer *par excellence*.

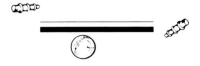

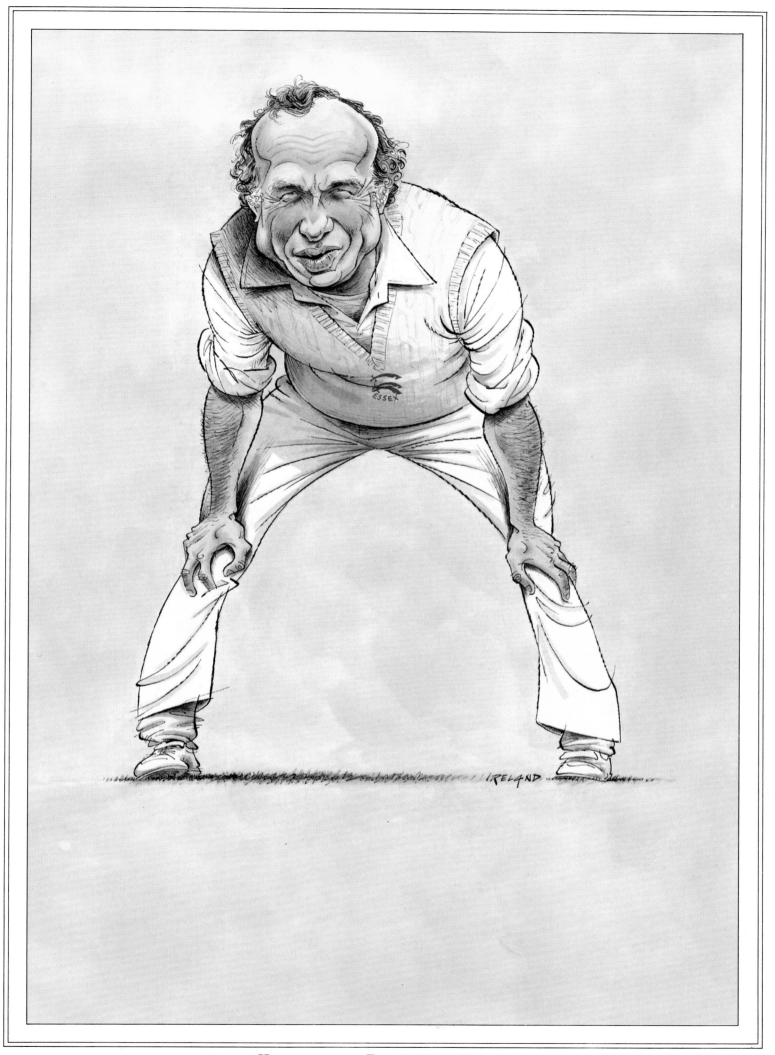

KEITH FLETCHER

FOR A LONG TIME Mike Gatting was given a raw deal by England captains. Now he is captain himself. Ironically indeed it was the captain who showed most faith in him whom he reluctantly ousted and eclipsed. Cricket can be a mean as well as a rewarding profession.

Great players usually get selected for their country at an early age. Gatting was selected at 20 but he was at once and for many years continued to be the expendable 'utility' man in the England batting order, never sure if he would be playing or, if he was, where he would be batting. In 1981 he did at last have a settled series, but three years later still seemed close to failure as a Test cricketer when twice falling lbw without playing a shot in the Lord's Test.

When the selectors sat down at the end of that season to choose their side for the tour to India, David Gower, who had taken over the captaincy from the naturally lugubrious Bob Willis, insisted not only that Gatting should be in his side but that he should be his vice-captain as well. As Mike Brearley's successor at Middlesex, Gatting already had experience of leadership. Indeed he had done outstandingly well as captain of the Sydney Grade side, Balmain.

'Gatt', as he has been known throughout the cricket world, thrived on the responsibility in India. He quickly became the side's leading batsman, scoring his first Test century at Bombay in his 54th innings for England and finishing the series with 575 runs at an average of 95. More than this, he became the team's driving force, an ebullient extrovert and the ideal foil to the quietly undemonstrative Gower.

Gower shared the accolades with Gatting when England came back from defeat in the first Test to win the series and enjoyed a personal triumph as both captain and batsman against Australia in 1985. Life then dealt him an unplayable hand in a series in the Caribbean.

In the early weeks of this fateful tour, Mike Gatting had looked the one England batsman capable of dealing for long with the constant barrage of West Indian fast bowling. In fact, on poor pitches, no-one could do so. Gatting received first a bouncer on the nose from Marshall which crushed it to pulp; then, after a difficult operation, a broken thumb. He therefore played in only one Test and emerged mentally if not physically less scarred than many of his mates. More important, perhaps, he had not shared in the full ignominy of England's nil-five defeat. After one Test of 1986 he was appointed to succeed Gower as captain and in Australia the following winter he led England on a most successful campaign.

His chunky, even porky, build encourages his admirers to think of him as being of the British Bulldog breed. He certainly is tough, and it is true that he relishes a fight. His greatest quality as a batsman is his assertiveness. He likes to get on top and when he does so he moves at full sail towards the enemy bowling, blasting off his main guns at them like some latter-day Elizabethan privateer. Pummelling drives, rasping square-cuts, meaty hooks and pulls are all Gatting specialities. Spinners, especially, quake within when he marches to the crease, narrow eyes gleaming, square jaw jutting, his brawny, butcher's arms flexed and ready.

A viandary analogy is not inappropriate. 'Gatt' has to be careful not to become 'Fat Gatt'. He has a gargantuan appetite but he makes up for it by throwing himself with maximum, boisterous energy into anything he does, on or off a cricket field. He is an outstanding catcher and a confident, assertive and genuinely useful medium-paced bowler. Above all, by believing so fully in himself, he has enabled those around him in the England team to believe in themselves too.

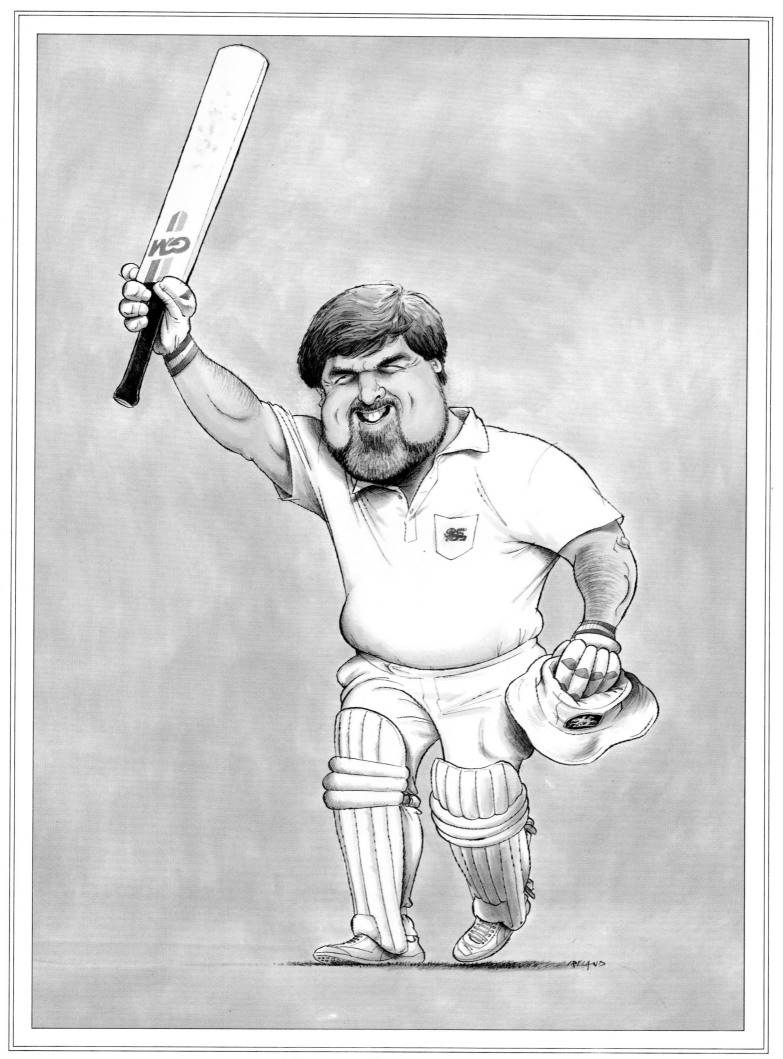

MIKE GATTING

WHETHER SUNIL GAVASKAR is the second greatest batsman of the Test match era after Bradman depends, amongst many things, on your definition of 'great'. Statistics, despite Mark Twain's definition, do not all lie and it is a fact that Gavaskar was the first man to score 30 Test centuries and the first past 10,000 Test runs. As he said at the time: 'Others may follow, but although others have also climbed Everest it is Hilary and Tensing we remember.'

Like Bradman, Gavaskar is little more than a Tom Thumb. Unlike the Don, however, there was never even the remotest suggestion that his nerve ever failed him against the armies of tall and muscular fast bowlers who hurled thunderbolts at him for 20 years. He repulsed them by means of a stout heart, a profound determination to succeed for himself and his country, and a batting technique of purest orthodoxy.

Unlike Geoff Boycott, who challenged him in his time for technical mastery, 'Sunny' could be a dasher as well as a blocker. A half-volley has always been a half-volley to him, first ball of a Test match or not. Of course a half-volley to Gavaskar might be a full-toss to a taller man; therefore he profited often from bowlers who pitched a little too short and so were cut and pulled and glanced with wristy skill, the brown eyes level behind the line of the ball.

He started in Test cricket with a flourish so brilliant that a lesser man would have dazzled himself and been unable to keep it up. His scores against the West Indies in that series of 1970–71 – in the Caribbean, mark you, though at a time when pitches were truer and fast bowlers not quite as plentiful as now – were 65, 67 not out, 116, 64 not out, 1, 117 not out, 124 and 220 not out. The world learned a new name.

The Indians themselves have seen a high proportion of his long, patient, match-winning or, more often, match-saving innings. But it is difficult to believe that they saw him achieve perfection for as long as he did when batting over eight hours without a flaw to score 221 at The Oval in 1979. Never once during this amazing innings were his feet in the wrong position and thus he was never less than perfectly balanced for every shot he played. He was out flinging the bat, after turning certain defeat for India into a possible victory.

Adored like a God throughout the Sub-Continent, though sometimes a prey to local jealousies, he has yet managed to keep a private life in Bombay, close always in spirit to his family. His uncle was a Test player and his sister married another. Sometimes, his fuse has blown in private; on the cricket field only once or twice. Generally he has been a dignified man as well as a dignitary.

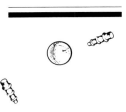

SUNIL GAVASKAR

A N ENGLAND SELECTOR once said an unkind thing to me about Graham Gooch, at a time when he had not yet fulfilled in Test cricket the huge promise of all his other cricket. I will paraphrase his comment into 'He's as soft as putty.' In the sense of soft-hearted, gentle or kind, he might have been right. If, however, he meant pusillanimous, he was wrong and Gooch has proved him so, not only by standing up without a flinch to the fastest bowlers – indeed it is usually they who have to flinch – but also by having the moral courage to play where he thinks he legitimately may and not to apologize for doing so. I refer, of course, to his visit to South Africa.

Gooch made the trip at a time when he knew it would not interfere with his commitments to anyone else. He did not believe he was doing wrong, or 'supporting a racist regime'; therefore he did not withdraw when some others did. He was voted captain by his fellow-players, although Geoffrey Boycott had been, until then, the leader of the band. They were well paid for the cricket they played and there was nothing particularly honourable about the trip, but nor was there anything dishonourable or illegal.

Gooch became, however, the chief target for those who strongly felt that he had done more than just ignore a TCCB warning not to go. He served a three-year sentence of no international cricket along with those who had toured with him, but remained *persona non grata* in the eyes of some politicians, some of them sincere men, others bigoted hypocrites, partly because of his reluctantly assumed leading role and partly because he had the honesty to say that *in exactly the same circumstances* he would make the same decision. He subsequently toured the West Indies against his better judgment and although he did not do himself full justice he played the best innings of the tour. That most cricket followers of any colour bore him no personal animosity was evident from the enthusiasm and generosity with which his success on that occasion, a One-Day International in Port of Spain, was received.

In a mood such as he was in that day there are few sights in modern cricket to equal the one of Gooch in full sail. He hits the ball very hard indeed, with a heavy bat brought down from a high backlift. His stance, with the head sideways and the eyes level, has annoyed the purists but should not have done because it is designed to keep him side-on to the ball; to suggest that he is wrong not to pick the bat up in the accepted way is to ignore the power with which he dismisses the bad ball from his presence like a horse's tail dealing with a persistent fly. Almost all his big innings in Test cricket have been memorable to watch, marked by fierce driving and bold hooking.

His bowling tends to be underrated. He always seems to be able to swing the ball at brisk medium and, what is more, he can move it both ways. He is a very reliable fielder, especially at second slip, and when he took a voluntary winter off to stay with his wife after the birth of twins to add to their eldest daughter, he kept himself very fit by training with West Ham United.

Time will tell how good a captain he may be. He has certainly started well with Essex. He has always been one of the dressing-room boys, but he seemed to take on the responsibility of making hard decisions without losing any friends. His sense of humour must help in that – and his soft heart.

GRAHAM GOOCH

WHAT WILL BE THE ULTIMATE verdict on David Ivon Gower? A minor genius, as Mike Brearley claimed him to be; or a flawed hero, as most with genius are? An aesthetic joy; or a batsman who wasted too much of his God-given talent? A captain who failed; or one who, sent on an impossible expedition, returned bloody but unbow'd?

There would be supporters for both sides of each question. But no-one, at least, would deny his immense and natural dignity through thick and thin.

He fell like a benison on the colourless and cultureless wasteland of English batsmanship in the late 1970s. Snub-nosed, curly-haired, boyish, willowy, smiling, he brought to the scene of first county and then, in 1978, only a year after the arrival of Ian Botham to English Test cricket, a grace which had been missing since Graveney, Cowdrey, May and Dexter.

Here again, at last, was a batsman of gay spontaneity; above all, instinctive, in the way that Denis Compton was when he first charmed his way onto the cricket scene just before the war. Unfettered as yet by the complexities of professional cricket, its technical obsessions and often safety-first strategies, Gower saw the ball early, moving languidly and with an almost visible smile of anticipation to persuade it away to leg with a caress, lean on it like a poplar in the wind to send it humming past cover, rock languidly back to pull it through mid-wicket, or cut it with the consummate ferocity of a crusader's sword.

There was, indeed, a real gallantry about the young Gower's play. Alone amongst his contemporaries he was instantly memorable. No-one could forget seeing him for the first time. My time was one early summer day at Grace Road, Leicester. He only made about 18, as many runs as his age, and his innings was over in a brief, dazzling flurry of strokes. Like a pretty young flirt whirling her skirts and flashing a smile before moving swiftly on, he had invited you to come back for more.

A world-weariness gradually and no doubt inevitably overtook him. Cricket became more a profession than a game, though his puppyish desire for fun has never really deserted him. But crowds and critics and selectors become impatient with youthful indiscretions. He had to buckle down; become the mature Test player; get his head over the ball for long periods; fight it out on grey mornings when wise fast bowlers constantly attacked him outside his off-stump, knowing the human way in which he could not resist temptation.

There were and are days when such bowlers, however good, suffer; when his almost godlike supremacy returns. Australia's bowlers in England in 1985 will no doubt say to their dying day that Gower was the best player they ever bowled at. He made 732 runs in nine Test innings, and a century against them for Leicestershire to boot. Even in the West Indies a few months later, when all his recent triumphs were so quickly revealed to be crumbling, like an Empire gone soft, he was England's most effective batsman. And the ready smile and at least exterior calm never left him.

Gower the man may have lost the unaffected innocence of youth, but his final record will still confirm his ability. Those who have watched him will know he was something special.

DAVID GOWER

THERE WAS MUCH consternation in the ranks of the 1987 Pakistan touring team to England when the team's vice-captain, Javed Miandad, failed to arrive for the start of the tour, because his wife was about to give birth to their second child. The moment he arrived the team looked a more formidable proposition, for he had been for many years one of the world's great batsmen, a bandy-legged buccaneer who had made 14 Test hundreds and nearly 6,000 runs before the age of 30.

Javed hails from Karachi, where his father journeyed before Partition in 1947, leaving the employ of the Maharajah of Palanpur in Gujerat to become secretary of the Muslim Gymkhana Club. Miandad and his four brothers all played for the club and word of the wiry little genius spread as quickly as his individual achievements. He scored a triple hundred at the age of 17 and was included in Pakistan's team in the 1975 World Cup in England, where his leg-spin bowling was as effective as his batting. (It has seldom been so since.) He quickly became a wanted man on the lists of several counties seeking an overseas player and performed prodigious feats for Sussex 2nd XI. At 19 he made a Test double hundred against New Zealand. At 24 he became captain of Pakistan. At 27 he became the youngest man to score 5,000 Test runs.

As a Test captain he has not, so far, been a success. He is a live-wire, inclined to hot-headedness, and he has too often incurred the wrath of opponents, as well as their admiration for the brilliance of his strokeplay. He came close to a stand-up fight with Dennis Lillee in one Test in Australia and in another ran out another man with a short fuse, Rodney Hogg, when he had played the ball defensively and gone for a walk to do some gardening. On another occasion in Sri Lanka he walked into the crowd, after he had been out, to deal personally with someone who had been giving him spurious advice.

Such rashness has sometimes afflicted his batting, for all his prodigious scoring. In one Test against Sri Lanka he was 92 not out when he noticed the long-off fieldsman still walking to his place with his back to the wicket as the bowler moved in. Down the pitch went Miandad to hit the ball over long-off. He missed and was stumped. He remains a passionate man who, for example, likes to do especially well in Faisalabad because this is where he met and married his wife.

Gradually, however, the dash and adventure of his game has started to mellow with experience, losing some of its scintillation in the process but making it in some ways more formidable still. He does not, for instance, play the reverse sweep so often these days, though he has used the shot with impish brilliance and great success, having first seen it played by Mushtaq and Hanif. When playing it he has always reminded me of those brilliant Pathan squash players who are able to change the direction of their shot with a deft turn of the wrist at the moment of impact, thus wrong-footing their opponents. Miandad is from the same brilliant sporting stock as the squash world champion Jehangir Khan.

As his ardour cools he should be more successful when the challenge of captaincy returns. If he goes on playing long enough, he may well surpass Gavaskar and Boycott as the highest Test scorer of all.

JAVED MIANDAD

THERE IS ABOUT BOTH the batting and the demeanour of Dean Jones a timeless quality which would fit into any era of the game. He has worn the baggy green cap with more genuine pride and commitment than anyone in a rather grim period for his country's cricket, exacerbated by the poaching of leading players by South Africa and a superfluity of one-day cricket, the legacy of the Packer years.

Jones himself suffered from playing too much limited-overs cricket and from being considered by short-sighted selectors as simply a one-day specialist. By the end of the 1986–87 season, in which he played magnificently against England after a hesitant start, he had played 45 times for Australia in 'Internationals' but only 10 times in Test matches.

As a youngster in Melbourne he was considered by many to be too brash for his own good, although his talent as a stylish, aggressive right-handed batsman and brilliant fielder was recognized widely. People sometimes forget that confidence in a batsman is never a bad thing. Tempered with a bit of experience and realism, and supported by a genuine talent, it can in fact be devastating and this Jones frequently was in the long summer of 1986–87 as he topped Australia's Test averages with 511 runs in 10 innings and then outscored everyone

in the one-day games as well, his 623 runs in 13 innings including three quite brilliant hundreds.

Tall, lean and strong, he is a dazzlingly quick mover on his feet and a bold driver, who hits equally well off the back foot. His runs against England were, in the end, in a losing cause, but one has the feeling that he may wreak a horrible revenge, assuming he recovers from the serious knee injury suffered at the end of the season during a friendly game of Rules football.

He has already shown his resilience in adversity. In the West Indies in his first Test he came in at 85 for five and put on a hundred with Allan Border. But three years later he was still unestablished and considered to be both a little too rash and a little too brash when he went out to bat in intense humidity against India at Madras. He had scored only 65 Test runs before this innings but, fighting dehydration and frequent nausea for the best part of two days he scored 210, an immortal contribution to only the second tied Test in history. He was too ill to field and spent much of the rest of the match in hospital fed by a saline drip.

Such stories prove that the romance of Test cricket lives on, even in the 1980s. Dean Jones seems sure to become one of the game's next folk-heroes.

DEAN JONES

IT IS NEVER EASY TO DECIDE how much the style of a cricket team owes to its captain and how much to the players under his command. It depends, of course, on the strength of the captain. Clive Lloyd's detractors say that he simply wound up his four fast bowlers and let them go, changing them round almost like workers on a shift system; and that he made little attempt to curb or calm them if, as was not infrequently the case, they were bowling too short too often; the end in his view apparently justifying the means.

His supporters were far more numerous. They recognized him as the man who enabled West Indian cricket to grow, at last; whose phlegmatic temperament, cool brain and natural dignity made those under him calmer in a crisis; better organized, and able to make the most of their abundant talents far more consistently than before.

If Lloyd as a captain did have a ruthless streak, which cannot be denied, he was not alone in that, nor was it surprising in view of his difficult start in the job. At one point the West Indies played 18 Tests in four years and won none. In Australia in 1975–76, even with Roberts and an immature Holding, his team were beaten 5–1. It did not happen again. The big money available during and after the two seasons of World Series Cricket concentrated the minds and bodies of Clive Lloyd and his team. Garner and Croft joined Roberts and Holding; later came Marshall. Fine fast bowlers such as Daniel, Clarke and Davis could not get a regular game. Clive Lloyd's West Indies were fitter and faster than any previous Caribbean team; except on a raging turner they were unbeatable.

Lloyd the captain tended in the latter part of his career to overshadow Lloyd the batsman, fielder and occasional medium-paced bowler, though he held many a fine catch and played an increasingly valuable role as the middle-order ballast in a side whose batting was never as strong as its bowling.

As a young man Lloyd was one of the greatest entertainers. An explosive left-handed hitter, driving with marvellous power, turning good-length balls into half-volleys, hitting boundaries, as John Arlott once said, with the ease of a man 'knocking off thistle-tops with a walking stick'. A Test hundred by Lloyd was always memorable; a hundred in a one-day match (and on the big occasion, especially at Lord's, he usually got one) almost guaranteed that his side would win.

His fielding was fantastic, long legs and telescopic arms taking him to the ball in an instant; and he could throw on target from the most unlikely places. A deadly cover-point became in time a brilliant slip.

Underneath all this success lay a great depth of character. Behind the scenes Frank Worrell, one gathers, could have his flashpoints, and Viv Richards is known to have them on the field. But Lloyd, apparently, never lost that scholarly calm. In triumph he was modest, and after setbacks dignified. He was not just supercat, but cool cat.

CLIVE LLOYD

I T TOOK THE REST of the world too long to appreciate the vivid flower of cricketing talent which for years blushed unseen in Sri Lanka. Duleep Mendis was fortunate to be reaching his peak when a long period of cricket diplomacy ended with the admittance of his country into full membership of the ICC. His own batting, notably in a brilliant innings which enabled Sri Lanka to defeat the England touring team in 1976–77 in a one-day match, had done much to prove to many doubters that the island really did contain players of Test class.

A Christian, he was born to the purple in one sense, his father having given him two famous cricketing names – Duleep after Duleepsinjhi, and Rohan after Kanhai. He quickly established himself in Sri Lankan schools cricket which has always been the strong base of the game in Ceylon. In 1972 he captained St Thomas's in the traditional encounter with Royal College and scored 184 out of 286 for nine. In three years of these matches he scored a record 386 runs at an average of 96.

He continued to break records and set trends. He played in Sri Lanka's inaugural Test, against England in Colombo, became his country's second captain, and led the island to their first Test victories, against India and Pakistan in the same 1985–86 season. He reached his first Test hundred with a six, against India at Madras in 1982–83 and promptly followed this with 105 in the second innings.

When he led the side to England in 1984 their form was unimpressive going into their first Test match at the headquarters of cricket. Yet thanks mainly to Sidath Wettimuny, who compiled a flawless 190, and to Mendis himself, England were embarrassed and soon forced to have no higher ambition than a draw.

Duleep played a dazzling innings of 111, taking the attack to the England bowlers on a slow wicket with the panache of a well-armed pirate taking on an unprepared merchant ship. It grew very grey on the second evening and the umpires offered Mendis the opportunity to go off for bad light. Sad to say, the majority of other Test captains would have needed no second invitation. Mendis could not understand what they were fussing about. He tore into Ian Botham, hooking him three times into the Tavern or the Mound for six, and reached his century off only 112 balls. In the second innings he was within one hit of becoming the second man in history to hit hundreds in each innings of a Lord's Test. The shot which would have taken him there fell a few yards short into the hands of deep mid-wicket.

He has had his low points as well. His technique is not without its faults and his desire to attack does not always pay such handsome dividends. Inevitably Sri Lanka have struggled in many of their Test matches and predictably much blame has been laid at the captain's door. But this podgy, bright-eyed, courteous, aquiline-nosed batsman has helped his country to do much better much more quickly than informed observers would have expected.

DULEEP MENDIS

DEREK RANDALL is a father now, with business interests. His benefit year is already behind him. But he looks as though he ought still to be wearing shorts, with ink stains on his fingers and one of his school socks down by his ankles, the other only half-covering a muddy knee.

Whoever first called him Pinocchio got it just right because, apart from his permanent little-boy look, his limbs seem to move like a puppet's, unencumbered by the normal limits imposed by bone and muscle. He has relinquished his right to be Nottinghamshire's regular cover-point – now Tim Robinson has assumed that role – but he still sprints and dives to make stops and catches which not only seem but actually are impossible for the average cricketer. With the possible exceptions of Colin Bland and the young Clive Lloyd he has been the most brilliant, exciting cover fielder of the last generation, a constant source of delight to spectators and as threatening to batsmen as a mamba in the grass.

Randall the batsman now employs the two-eyed stance once used amongst others by Barrington, Parks and Titmus. It helps him to work the ball into the gaps on the legside with even more dexterity than in his youth, when he preferred the full-blooded boundary to the carefully stroked one or two. But, give him anything like a half-volley on the off-stump and he will cream it through the covers all along the ground with a text-book purity. And, having seen the ball bounce back off the fence, he can no more resist a quick conversation with his batting partner now than he could as a nervous twenty year-old.

Randall has to chat to someone – partner, umpire, opposing bowler – anyone within range. In the field he will find a spectator to talk to as well if there is one in range. He so wants them to enjoy it all as much as he does. No wonder they love him so at Trent Bridge.

I have been lucky enough to see most of the lows and highs of Derek's career. He was admirably stoic when he completely lost his form and confidence on one tour of Australia. But he was a hero with a capital H at Melbourne in 1977 and at Sydney two years later. Some people, mostly those who were not there, discount the latter match-winning century at the SCG as though Hogg, Hurst, Yardley, Higgs and Dymock amounted to an attack that was not first-class. That simply is not true.

It is certainly true, however, that nothing he has done or ever will do can quite compare with the glory of the Centenary Test. Everyone will recall, no doubt, that after England and Australia had bowled each other out absurdly cheaply, and Australia had then made a big second-innings score, there was an awful possibility that England, tired after their long tour of India, would succumb a second time to end a truly great occasion in premature and embarrassing anti-climax. Her Majesty The Queen, due on the last day of the game after opening her Australian Parliament in Canberra, was in danger of arriving after the game had finished. The Nottinghamshire imp saved the day. Hooking and cutting and driving and, of course, chatting, he stole the show – from The Queen and Dennis Lillee and everyone else.

He has been through many vicissitudes since that day of inspiration – and enjoyed plenty of triumphs too. And Retford's most famous son will know to the day he dies that they cannot take that achievement away. The self-deprecating, slightly barmy youngster who had made his first mark on his first MCC tour by turning a cartwheel during a stuffy soft-drinks reception to the amazement and amusement of his Indian hosts, was suddenly a national hero. The pleasure he gave then and has often given since will long survive his career.

DEREK RANDALL

PROUD AS A PEACOCK, handsome as a prince, strong as a horse, Viv Richards was for the best part of ten years recognized as the best batsman in the world. That is a big statement. There were other claimants, and times when he did not live up to his almost impossibly high reputation. But it is safe to say that for a decade after his blossoming in 1976 no-one would have picked a World XI without him.

He was not as consistent as other great players, but when the chips were down he dominated. No bowler in any conditions was too good for him. His record bears close examination, but it is the way in which he scores his runs, always with his team rather than himself his first priority, which sets him apart. He hits immensely hard and plays every shot known to man from a basic technique which is orthodox. Indeed, no-one's forward defensive stroke is played with a bat which seems broader. Lately he has become more unorthodox, adding to his tendency to work the ball off the stumps through mid-wicket a liking for the 'Sunday League shot', the cover drive played to a ball on the leg-stump with the feet well outside the stumps and the blade coming inside out. Nevertheless some of his most memorable innings have been played in the limited-overs game. Three centuries in finals at Lord's come to mind; and the extraordinary *tour de force* at Old Trafford in 1984, when he scored 189 not out off 170 balls with five sixes and 21 fours, making 93 of a last-wicket partnership of 106 in 14 overs.

Recently his career has entered a new and challenging phase. He has been given his cards by Somerset after helping them to win trophies for the first time in their history and has followed many other great West Indians into the Lancashire League. More significantly, perhaps, he has taken over the captaincy of the West Indies and, after emulating Clive Lloyd by leading them to a five-nil 'blackwash' of England, he tasted defeat in Tests in Pakistan and New Zealand, not to mention in one of Australia's annual series of limited-overs games when the West Indies failed for the first time to win the 'World Series' tournament.

People were saying after this difficult winter of 1986–87 that there was more to it than just the gradual decline of an ageing team; that Richards's temperament and his failure to get the best out of his men were also to blame. If people had pointed to his failure to bat at his best, and the resultant unaccustomed pressure on the batsmen around him, they might have been nearer the mark. Whether his own decline was temporary or permanent, time would tell, but I should be very surprised if he were not to come storming back.

I first saw Richards – 'Vivi' rather than 'Viv' he was then to Antiguans – marauding an England attack at St John's Recreation Ground, just before he signed for Somerset. He was brilliant and carefree and the whole island seemed to be bouncing up and down with joy as his marvellous natural talent expressed itself in a volley of fours and sixes. He was a sterner, less innocent man by the time that, purely through the extraordinary achievements of Richards and his compatriot and contemporary, Andy Roberts, Antigua was granted a regular Test match.

He seemed to consider it a matter of duty to score a hundred when England first played a Test there in 1981. Five years later he was captain of the West Indies and scored another one – off 56 balls. No-one had scored a century in fewer balls in a Test, but he was quite unaware of his record at the time. What he wanted was to declare as quickly as possible. So he treated a tired but reputable England attack like schoolgirls. When he has really wanted something, 'Smoking Joe' has always had the power to go out and get it.

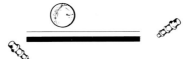

VIV RICHARDS

OF ALL THE GREAT batsmen of his era Zaheer Abbas was probably the least vaunted, and as a character the one who least looked for the adulation and wealth which are generally the reward for someone who scores centuries out of habit.

He made 12 hundreds for Pakistan: more, and at a higher average than anyone except Javed Miandad, and 107 in his 21-year career. In seven matches, uniquely, he scored a hundred in both innings. Yet throughout he looked like a student who had accidentally strayed onto a cricket field, stayed out of curiosity and, on finding one side a player short, decided to have a go.

Appearances are not wholly deceptive. Although no academic, his approach to cricket itself was distinctly studious and the quiet reserved manner he had at the crease was typical of him wherever he was. Devotion to the rigid disciplines of the Moslem religion has kept him sober and intense. He was never at home in a hotel bar; his only home was in Karachi with his wife and daughters. He had been born around the time of Partition, a worrying period for everyone on the Sub-Continent, and his father, a locust-controller, had been obliged to retreat to safe ground. Although Zaheer was destined to travel the world and to spend much of his life based in Bristol, his heart was always with his family.

Perhaps a certain isolation forged within him the deep concentration which enabled him to bat for long periods match after match. He was never physically robust but mentally he was unbreakable and records had a distinct appeal for him. Although he was vulnerable against good seam bowlers in some conditions, one wonders how many more records he might have broken had he been an opening batsman.

Unlike some prolific scorers he was never dull to watch. Tall, slender and balanced, he played his strokes with a wristy elegance, controlling the high bouncing ball with strong, flexible wrists. He hit most beautifully off the back foot through the offside, or off the front foot through mid-wicket, always leaning on and stroking the ball, never bludgeoning it. Cardus said of Reggie Spooner that he used his bat as a lady would use a fan. Zaheer had that same air of composure and delicacy. He was an artist, but less temperamental than most: an artist combined with a scientist, in fact; a formidable combination.

ZAHEER ABBAS

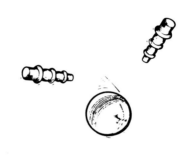

THE ALL-ROUNDERS

EVEN DIEHARD CRICKET enthusiasts can get a little blasé, in the age of over-indulgence in international cricket, and over-exposure of the star players, when a Richards or a Border, a Lloyd or a Gower comes out to bat. But with Ian Botham it simply is not so. The most hard-bitten critic gets as big a thrill of anticipation as the most starry-eyed schoolboy when this human oak tree surges out of the pavilion bare-headed and belligerent, a brawny right arm swinging his huge chunk of a bat in fearsome circles.

Warts and all, Ian Botham is irresistible, the biggest hitter since Arthur Wellard and, before him, Gilbert Jessop but in a quite different class from Wellard and more consistent even than Jessop. If he had never taken a wicket, Ian Botham would surely be recognized as a great cricketer. Yet as I write he is the highest wicket-taker in the history of Test cricket and, to top all this, he has taken some of the most brilliant imaginable catches at second slip where he stands, large hands resting on tired knees, eyes steady, waiting to grasp any victim who happens to have eluded his own attempts to dismiss him with booming away-swingers or deliberately tempting bouncers.

Many a sporting champion has been to some extent the victim of his own success and Ian is no exception. He has performed such super-human feats for his country that people tend to expect them every time, forgetting that he is not in fact superhuman, merely *primus inter pares*. You could argue that he is England's best all-rounder since W.G.,

though cases could be made for, amongst others, Wally Hammond, Frank Woolley and Wilfred Rhodes. He is most certainly the best since the war, the superior of both Bailey and Greig, and it is difficult to think of any player in England's Test history who has so successfully combined effectiveness with entertainment.

The basis of his game is attack. He wants to be on top from the first ball he bowls and the first one he faces. Very often he is. Cricket is all about taking the initiative and this is one reason for his amazing achievements. Others are his huge natural ability, his strength, and his boisterous courage.

For a season or two in the late 1970s Ian Botham was as good a fast-medium swing bowler as there has been, though perhaps he never had quite the same control as Barnes, Tate or Bedser. Maurice Tate could bat a bit, of course, but not half as well as Botham. In fact only Jessop can be compared as a hitter good enough to turn a match in an hour of fierce assault. None of us who saw them will forget the centuries at Headingley and Old Trafford in 1981. They were 'such stuff as dreams are made on'.

Is he still the best all-rounder in the world? Does it matter much anyway? For what it is worth one would always put Hadlee, sometimes Kapil Dev and, when fit, Imran Khan ahead of him as bowlers, that is on Ian's form of the last three or four years. But, for all his sometimes outrageous lifestyle, he has more stamina and durability than any of these.

IAN BOTHAM

THEY CALLED HIM 'The Mantis' and he was well named. His long arms would stretch to take brilliant slip catches; his long legs carry him at a gentle trot to bowl innocuous-looking medium-paced floaters which nevertheless earned him many a major scalp in an important match; and, like a mantis, as a batsman he would be very patient in seeking his reward.

Jeremy Coney captained New Zealand with charm and intelligence in his last two years as a Test cricketer, keeping up the admirable momentum started by his predecessor Geoff Howarth and contributing most valuably to events both off the field and on it. He became the first man to captain New Zealand to victory in a series in England; and he finished by beating the West Indies at Christchurch, not a bad way to bow out before settling to life as a teacher, cricket commentator and family man.

As a batsman he was something of a late developer. Although he was always making useful contributions in his upright, correct, orthodox way, driving stylishly and hitting the ball straight off the back foot, he managed to play 131 innings in seven years between his fourth and fifth hundreds in first-class cricket. He made up for this by saving New Zealand from certain defeat

with his 174 not out at Wellington in the first Test of 1983–84 and he might have made many more runs had he been given more responsibility and a higher place in the batting order.

He was untroubled, however, by any intense personal ambition. Playing for his country was treated as a deep privilege and a way of seeing the world. He always gave the impression that he was enjoying himself on and off the field and he was an ideal ambassador for New Zealand. When, in the Lord's Test of 1986, England's wicket-keeper Bruce French was injured by a short ball from Richard Hadlee, Coney gave his permission for French to be replaced, for as long as they wished, by any specialist wicket-keeper not selected for the match.

It was an extraordinarily generous gesture considering that England had in their ranks a perfectly serviceable reserve 'keeper in Bill Athey. It gave the Lord's crowd, on the day that the Queen paid her traditional visit, the chance to see Bob Taylor keeping wicket for England again. It also showed that New Zealand cricket had lost any sense of inferiority. Coney, the valuable bits-and-pieces all-rounder and amiable, articulate skipper, was the man who consolidated his country's position close to the top of the cricketing tree.

JEREMY CONEY

IN THE YEARS OF THE middle-1980s – since, in fact, the retirement of Dennis Lillee – Richard Hadlee has been the greatest bowler in the world, a man as pre-eminent in his art as in their day were Spofforth or Barnes.

Like both those demons of other ages, Hadlee has a lean and hungry look; like them he is something more than dedicated; like them he seems fuelled by an inner drive as well as a strong, wiry body; like them he is an independent soul, who deals in his own way with the cricket authorities who employ him. Early in 1987 he became the first man to negotiate a contract to play for his country for a three-year period. It protected New Zealand from the possible poaching of Hadlee by South Africa or any would-be Kerry Packer imitator. It also ensured that New Zealand would remain close to the top of the international tree. For one may say of Hadlee as one may of few other cricketers of any era that any team he plays for becomes a quite different proposition, formidable by virtue of his brilliant bowling and potentially destructive batting.

New Zealand's fortunes have depended on Richard Hadlee to a quite remarkable degree. He lifted them from second-class to first-class with a succession of superb bowling performances. For Nottinghamshire he has been equally influential, committing himself heart and soul to the county's cause, enabling them to win their first Championship for 42 years. Three years later, in 1984, he became the only man to do the double since the number of Championship matches was reduced.

The other extraordinary feature of Hadlee's career has been the fact that, although most fast bowlers become less effective with age, he has become, apparently at least, better and better. When first he appeared he ran a long way to the wicket with a pronounced sway of the body both in his approach and his delivery. The long, unruly dark hair signified the waywardness of youth.

Gradually a sterner man evolved, a calculating bowler with command of every nuance of the art of swing and spin. His run-up became shorter; fierce and direct, with little time wasted in useless demonstrativeness, every ounce of energy going into the delivery from a high, rhythmic action, the right wrist locked behind the ball at the key moment so that it landed time and again on the seam, to whip away sharply towards the slips or dart back angrily at the batsman like a striking cobra.

By equal dedication allied to natural ability inherited from and shared with one of the greatest of cricketing families, Richard turned himself from a tailend left-hander into a genuine batsman, a furious driver who can turn the course of a match by bold, incisive hitting.

He likes to amuse his colleagues at Trent Bridge with an excellent impersonation of Basil Brush's laugh, but single-minded devotion to physical fitness and the improvement of his game have not been without personal cost. He has had to rely for moral support on an understanding wife, and in the months after his double in 1984 he became so depressed by the unyielding demands of round-the-year cricket that he was close to nervous breakdown. He yearned for a more normal family life and the regularity of a nine-to-five job. Being a champion, he discovered, is tough. But he has never let himself, his family or his country down.

RICHARD HADLEE

ONE IS TEMPTED TO PUN: is there anything Imran Khannot? He has played his cricket, during a long and very illustrious career, with the bearing of a prince, hovering between overt haughtiness and innate pride. He has a tremendous presence on a cricket field, batting and bowling with an air of superiority to all those around him. Whenever he is in the Pakistan side he lends not just his individual talent, but also his unshakable optimism. His is the confidence not of the braggart or the swank, but of a man who believes profoundly in his own God-given ability. He never expects to be beaten or bettered.

His brilliant all-round talent was obvious from his schooldays, begun in Lahore and finished, briefly, at RGS Worcester. He was outstanding at Oxford, though not as good a leader of lesser mortals as his cousin Majid Khan had been at Cambridge.

He developed swiftly after his university days, his experience broadened by cricket first for Worcestershire and later, after a move inspired by an affair of the heart, for Sussex. His physique broadened too, enabling him to become one of the fastest bowlers in the world, with a vigorous, athletic action culminating in a magnificent final leap. When he began his second tour as Pakistan's captain in England, in 1987, he needed only 10 more wickets to join the short, if growing, list of those who have taken 300 Test wickets.

His batting is orthodox, impressive, confident, cool-headed and classy. He hits the ball exceptionally hard. Yet he has scored rather less heavily, on the whole, than one might have expected, partly no doubt because he has always had so many talented specialist batsmen ahead of him in the order.

He has an extraordinary effect on the fair sex, many of whom would do anything to catch his eye. In the World Series years in Australia the publicity wallahs made a point of building up his film-star image, a personality cult to which Imran himself did not object, though he did not go looking for it. Girls, and the playboy image, came naturally to him, fell into his lap you might say. When he was on tour for Pakistan, the groundsman at Hove rejoiced for it meant a considerable reduction in the phone-calls from unknown females asking for 'Immy's' telephone number.

He has been an outstanding Test captain, tactically shrewd and happy to lead by example. Pakistan were half the side without him when he was absent for a while with a serious injury to his shin caused by jarring of the front leg as it pounded down on hard grounds in his explosive delivery. But when he returned he did not spare himself as the main strike bowler. For many years Sarfraz Nawaz had been his most regular opening partner, but late in his career he discovered a potentially even better bowler than Sarfraz in the whippy left-armer Wasim Akram. It enabled Imran to bowl within himself at times, conserving himself for bursts of real speed when the time was ripe.

He has not always been the most gracious of losers, being inclined to give umpires the sharp end of a piercing tongue at the end of a match or series. He knows the value of a good quote in the newspapers when Pakistan's performance has disappointed him and his followers at home. But he has been, nonetheless, an adornment to the game and his country's greatest all-round player bar none.

IMRAN KHAN

THERE IS SOMETHING reminiscent of a wild animal in the sight of Kapil Dev on the cricket field. He is a restless figure, erect and alert, saucer eyes darting hither and thither, muscles, it seems, twitching like a deer on the lookout for danger. But it is his opponents who need to beware, for attack not defence is Kapil's constant concern, and for a decade he has been one of the most compellingly exciting cricketers in the world.

He first made a mark as a fast bowler from the then rather unfashionable cricketing area of Haryana, a state he has put on the map in the same way that Richards and Roberts elevated Antigua. The art of pure fast bowling seemed to come naturally to him. He was swift without being lethally quick, but he has always possessed a natural away-swinger with his direct, almost military approach to the stumps after a slow walk-back, culminating in a glorious final leap during which the waiting batsman sees the whites of his eyes peeping from behind a high left arm.

Despite his almost stiff-looking back, straight as a shield, he fields brilliantly in any position. He has tended to stand close to the wicket in recent years since sharing the captaincy with the little maestro, Gavaskar.

His batting probably came as a pleasant surprise to those outside his home environment, for not many opening bowlers can also be matchwinners with a bat. Kapil has frequently turned the course of a match by bold, clean, supremely confident and fearless hitting. The drive is his special glory, either side of straight and struck with such force that it seldom matters if he hits the ball in the air. His timing, crisp as fresh lettuce, leaves fielders leaden-footed.

He has had some dramatic ups-and-downs as a Test captain, the first of the 'ups' being the 1983 World Cup success in England, made possible only through an extraordinary virtuoso performance by Kapil himself at the lovely Nevill Ground at Tunbridge Wells. There, before the banks of vivid rhododendrons, the underestimated Zimbabwe side had reduced the might of India to 9 for four when Kapil came out to bat. Soon they were 17 for five, but Kapil hit six sixes and sixteen fours in an innings of 175 not out. India won not only this match but the semi-final against England and the final against West Indies.

If any modern cricketer has had charisma, it is Kapil Dev. India may be inconsistent under his command, but they are no longer considered to be dull.

KAPIL DEV

GREG MATTHEWS WAS Australia's Player of the Year in 1985–86. When, at the start of the following season, Australia found themselves in trouble against England in the Brisbane Test, there was an extraordinary display of faith in his ability: up in the Press-box at The Gabba the assembled army of journalists, almost to a man, uttered statements of relief when they saw Matthews emerging from the pavilion at number seven.

He was the man to stop the rot, they felt. He duly made a fifty and by dogged batting and a good deal of talking managed to stave off a second successive defeat for Australia in the next game at Perth. But gradually his outer ebullience became crushed by inner doubts and by the end of the summer he was being viewed by the same disillusioned scribes as just another player in a country which had temporarily lost its grip on international cricket.

Matthews is a tough, useful, determined little cricketer; a steady, flat, off-spin bowler; a staunch, correct left-hand bat; and a brilliant fielder. He is also a cocky, slightly zany character, restless as a wave in a storm and irrepressible as a cuckoo in a clock. Some people think he is a show-off; others warm to his *joie-de-vivre*. He loves his cricket, works at it and thinks about it, and his breezy, brassy mien hides a serious professional. After a struggle to establish himself and a season of glory followed by one of disappointment, it will be interesting to see if he can sustain a promising start. It may be that he is not quite good enough in either of the game's main departments to make a lasting impact as a Test all-rounder.

Then again, it may be that the adulation he received during and after his deeds for New South Wales and Australia in his first full season in international cricket did him no good. The agents moved in, seeing in this bouncy little fellow with the punk hairstyle, who liked to shadow-box, break-dance, or contort his body into physical jerks whilst the ball was on its way back to the bowler, a very 'saleable commodity'. We have seen how some golfers go off the boil and lose their inner drive after winning a big tournament. It may have happened to Matthews, though unfortunately he is not so good that he can succeed in high company without giving his game everything he has, nor so rich that he can afford to slip too far.

But he still has a lot going for him: not a little talent, enthusiasm, and belief in himself. No doubt he can make those fickle fans and writers believe in him again.

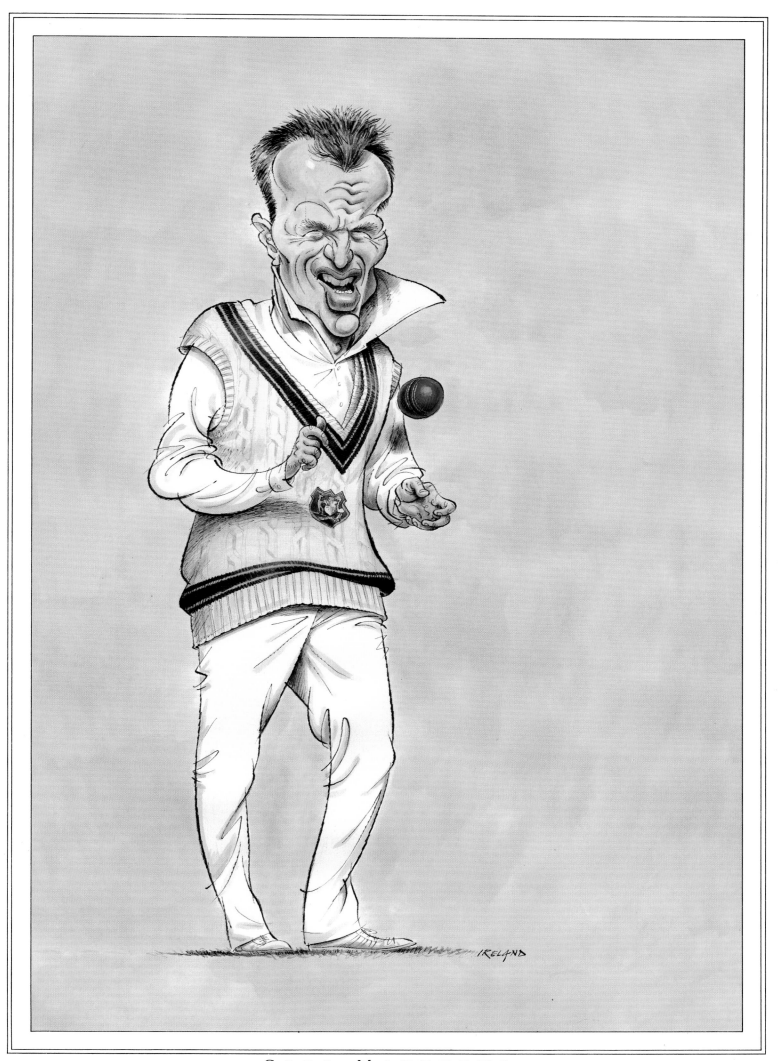

GREG MATTHEWS

THE WICKET-KEEPERS

FOR MANY YEARS the only Moslem in the Indian team, Syed Mujtaba Hussein Kirmani was a wicket-keeper of great polish and admirable consistency and a batsman of tremendous dash and invention.

He succeeded Farokh Engineer in the Indian team and shared in many triumphs, most notably the World Cup of 1983 when he was proud to be voted the best wicket-keeper in the competition. He is a man, as well as a cricketer, of much charm. One of his predecessors once apologized to an England batsman at a hotel after he had been given out to a dubious bat-pad catch. The wicket-keeper in question assured the batsman that he had not appealed, indeed considered him most unlucky to have been given out. The English cricketer went round the corner to buy an evening paper from the hotel lobby shop and there was a huge picture on the front page of the evening paper showing the same 'keeper leaping in the air in frantic appeal the second before the umpire raised his finger!

Kirmani was, in contrast, a sincere man. He appealed with the best of them, but would never have apologized for doing so. He took some brilliant catches himself, and some

dazzling stumpings. One of his best was down the legside off Prasanna to dismiss Roger Tolchard at an important moment of the Bombay Test in 1976–77. During this series he established himself as the best 'keeper in India and, with so much experience against the spinners, it is doubtful if Alan Knott or Rodney Marsh could have improved on his work.

His batting contributions were always good to watch: generally aggressive and often most valuable in a crisis. One could sense his enjoyment when he drove a fast bowler in low skims past mid-off or mid-on. Apart from two relatively unsuccessful tours of the West Indies, when his 'keeping was also disappointing, a series involving India never passed without Syed Kirmani making some telling contributions with the bat, including one Test hundred, which yielded an average in the mid-twenties at the highest level and proved his ability to wag the Indian tail.

He made a pilgrimage to Mecca halfway through his career for which he shaved off what remained of a receding hairline. The Kojak look suited him and he maintained it as a sort of trademark. One thinks of him, in fact, as a sparkling cricketer: shining pate, winning smile and glittering deeds with the gloves.

SYED KIRMANI

IT WAS SUPPOSED to have been a conversation between Rod Marsh, the likeable larrikin behind Australia's stumps for 15 years, and Graham, his equally chunky brother, which sowed one of the earliest seeds of the Packer Revolution. Graham, who spoke fewer words, favoured a short-back-and-sides appearance and modelled himself, so it always seems, on Gary Player, had made a small fortune out of golf; Rod eventually did so out of cricket. But when the conversation took place ('How much are you earning for that, Rod?' 'Oh, about five.' 'Is that five thousand?' 'No five hundred'), it was not easy for cricketers, even those as well established as Marsh, to make more than a 'comfortable', yet hard-earned living out of their sport.

Rod Marsh fared better with World Series Cricket. He became captain of his State, Western Australia. There were those who thought he ought also to have become captain of Australia. Now he is a competent television sports commentator, for Channel Nine, of course.

He was an exceptionally good, athletic, brave wicket-keeper although never as polished as a Tallon or an Oldfield. Perhaps if he had kept more regularly to spin bowlers he would have become so. Certainly he missed practically nothing standing back, hurling his scrum-half figure at edges off Lillee and Thomson which many a 'keeper would have left to slip, third-man or long-leg. He was tough as teak; never worrying about bruises or strains. With the bat he hit violently left-handed, though he was a better player when he tried to build an innings. Perhaps he did not work quite as hard on his batting technique as he should have done. But he was a good man to have around in a crisis, even if his brain did not always over-rule his heart.

He was intensely loyal to his team and his friends. He viewed foreigners, especially Poms, and extra-especially Pom journalists, with grave suspicion from behind his moustache. He was almost the archetype of Ian Chappell's fine Australian team which got a reputation for aggressive no-nonsense cricket on the field and sometimes graceless, rough, earthy behaviour off it. The reputation may have been exaggerated; it was certainly not completely unearned. Rod Marsh himself could always judge between right and wrong. There was a warm heart beneath the scowls; and he showed himself in a true light when he admitted that he had not caught Derek Randall towards the climax of the Melbourne Centenary Test, though the umpire had ruled the scooped-up catch as legitimate.

Rod was always a gambler. He had a punt on England at 500-to-1 against when Australia seemed certain to win the Headingley Test of 1981. But even if he had risked his home and family he would never have thrown a match for Australia. More recently he gave the bookies at Perth a fearful hammering with a bet made on impulse when rain stopped play in a match at his second home, the 'Waccer'. And when Paul Hogan and John Cornell came looking for 'godfathers' for a film project designed to boost Australia, he supported it willingly.

The film was *Crocodile Dundee*, which pulled in millions of dollars from all round the world. The hard-up Test 'keeper of the mid-Seventies had struck it rich, but apart from exchanging sweaty shirt and flannels for a smart blazer, tie and slacks, he had not changed.

RODNEY MARSH

IF THERE IS SOMETHING of the eternal schoolboy in all cricketers, there is more than most in Bob Taylor. He remained as skittish as a lamb when keeping wicket for Derbyshire past his fortieth birthday. He even got out of his civvies to take over behind the stumps during a Lord's Test after Bruce French had been injured by a bouncer from Richard Hadlee. He kept beautifully, of course.

In his time there was never a more polished wicket-keeper. The ball melted into his gloves. Nor was there a fitter one. By constant alertness and quick, neat movement of the feet, he was in the right place at the right time. Up to the stumps his hands moved to the ball, it seemed, by instinct, but 'instinct' was actually born of hard practice. Keeping back to the quick stuff he did not often need to fling himself about as lesser players do. He would gather in on two balanced feet the leg-glances which others might take, or miss, amidst a dive and a somersault.

He loved his cricket, would talk about it to anyone at any time. He was as proud of his last Test cap for England as he was of his first, gained somewhat controversially in New Zealand when Ray Illingworth at last took pity on him after his long-filled role as understudy to Alan Knott, whose batting was always superior and whose wicket-keeping sometimes had a genius and brilliance which even the quiet craftsman could not match. This was just Bob's misfortune, for he was a wicket-keeper of unblemished excellence and extraordinary consistency.

He set standards for all other understudies to follow. He was always in a state of readiness for the call which seldom came (for Knott himself was a fitness fanatic). He cheerfully accepted his lot without a mean word or even, it seemed, an envious thought. He did all the duties which reserves on tours are obliged to do: practise in the nets; fetch and carry for others; attend all the social functions.

Bob was so good at these that his team-mates called him 'Chat'. He was superb at the small-talk, be it with senior diplomats and political figures or with cricket-followers, some of them boring, out for a fortnight in the sun to support the England team in the middle of winter. This is one of the attributes of a gentleman: a consideration for others and a respect for them, however foolish or humble.

He was the same on the field. Gamesmanship and dissension were not words in his vocabulary. The game has changed almost beyond recognition since the likes of Ranji and C.B. Fry wrote about codes of behaviour in their books on cricket; but Bob would have agreed and complied with everything they said. He was in the timeless tradition of the best cricket professionals: not by any means a characterless yes-man, but a believer in traditions and standards.

Therefore when some of the players on an England tour late in his career got their priorities wrong, drinking and drug-taking to the detriment of their own game and the dishonour of their country, he was in a difficult position. He decided he did not want to tour with them again. He did not expose them personally but nor was he prepared to lie that such things had not been going on. Not a puritan, Bob Taylor, but certainly a man of virtue and sterling worth, proud of his profession and his country; not the only sort of man who won an Empire, but the sort without which that Empire would not have been won.

BOB TAYLOR

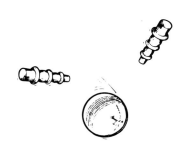

THE BOWLERS

THE BEST SPIN BOWLERS are often as full-blooded and wholehearted as the fiercest quick ones. Abdul Qadir is one of them. Not for him the slow, Laker-like stroll back to bowl, the comfortable amble to the crease, the ready acceptance of being hit for four, the cool calculation of a batsman's destruction. Instead Abdul is all emotion and commitment: hot-blooded, aggressive, restless.

He was born, it seems, to bowl leg-spin. Give him a cricket ball and he cannot resist tweaking it, strong fingers and wrists fizzing out miniature practice deliveries as he hastens back to his bowling mark. His bounding, energetic approach culminates in a twirl of arms and body so violent that it lifts him far off the ground as he follows through towards a batsman never quite sure if it is the leg-spinner, the top-spinner or one of at least two different googlies.

For years he has been much the best leg-break bowler in the world, indeed the only one frequently liable to win a Test match when Allah is with him. A gentle, relatively elderly Australian called Bob Holland had his successes during Qadir's time, but except on one occasion at Lord's his triumphs all came at his native Sydney where conditions suited him best. Then a young Indian called Sivaramakrishnan had a day of glory against England but he could not keep it up. Qadir, however, when in the mood and in the groove, worries the best batsmen on the best wickets. And like Doug Wright, England's outstanding leg-spinner either side of the last war, he is often *too* good for the batsman, fizzing it well past the edge of a groping or a flailing bat.

Sometimes, too, he goes over the top of the wicket, for generous bounce comes from that energy-packed action.

Near-misses provoke in him undisguised anguish. He leaps like a salmon or howls like a dervish. His appeals are frequent, fiery-eyed and zealous. He defies the umpire to disagree. Once he had Botham plumb in front with a full toss and looked as though he wished to take umpire Constant to special arbitration by General Zia-Ul-Haq for daring to question whether even as full-length a ball as this might have turned too much and missed the stumps. In the same series Derek Randall scored a hundred marked by frequent miscues against Qadir. It seemed he never had the slightest idea which way the ball was going to turn. Leg-spinners are seldom lucky.

A devout Moslem from a poor family in Lahore, he once insisted that the Pakistan Board should pay the mortgage on his house. He and the Board have by no means always seen eye to eye. He was sent home from New Zealand on one tour for disciplinary reasons, and has played fewer Tests than he should have done. But he has been an adornment to a game dominated in his era by fast bowlers, bringing an Oriental magic sometimes so potent that it is a wonder he does not arrive at matches on a carpet. All too seldom has he been able to bowl on pitches with enough pace and bounce in them to enable him to use his brilliant skills to the maximum; but he has kept the art of back-of-the-hand spin alive against the odds and one can only pray that he has inspired a generation of imitators.

ABDUL QADIR

LANCE CAIRNS PLAYED Test cricket for New Zealand for ten years. He toured England, Australia, India, Pakistan, New Zealand and Sri Lanka. In the Southern winter he would sometimes come over to England and play for Durham. Yet he never played cricket like a professional in the sense that it ever seemed for him anything more than a game, to be played hard but essentially for fun. As such he personified New Zealand cricket even in a period when, at least towards the end of Cairns's career, they were starting to get used to the unaccustomed idea of winning.

Cairns was born to the outdoors. Big and strong, he has hands as big as Alec Bedser's and looks as though he ought to have arrived at the cricket ground by horse, or perhaps by tractor.

Despite his strength he was a medium-paced bowler rather than a quick one, although he certainly hit the deck. Bowling with his weight almost on the wrong foot, front foot splayed and chest square to the batsman, he would swing it mainly in to the right-hander but sometimes the other way as well and he developed a genuine leg-cutter which Bedser himself would not have disowned. He bowled for long spells, perspiring freely but never giving in, often at his most courageous on the slow, unresponsive pitches of the Indian Sub-Continent. To be really effective, though, he liked humid conditions and a grassy pitch. In such conditions he inspired New Zealand to their first Test win in England by taking seven for 74 in the first innings and ten wickets in the match at Headingley in 1983.

In the same match Cairns contributed a brutal 24 not out with the bat. He had taken to using a heavy blade with sloping shoulders which in a Test match gave him even more the appearance of a blacksmith. He was a delighted hitter of the most enormous sixes, apt to get out caught whilst running a third. For Otago he once scored a century in 52 minutes, the fastest recorded in New Zealand. He had faced 45 balls. He made no bones about his tactics, gathering himself to hit the ball out of the ground as early and as often as possible.

In the team cause, however, he could and sometimes did resist the temptation to give himself and the crowd some fun. When he came to join Jeremy Coney in the first Test at Wellington the winter after that success at Headingley, New Zealand, although they were 402 for eight, looked sure to be beaten by England, who had been ahead by 244 on first innings. But Cairns survived an early scream for lbw and, perhaps incensed a little by the reaction of those around him, stayed to make 64 out of a record ninth-wicket partnership of 118. The match was drawn and New Zealand went on to win the series. Cairns himself had taken the first six wickets in England's innings.

During a tour Lance Cairns liked to get on a golf course if he possibly could. It does not need much imagination to see him giving the ball a fearful belt. He was a rugger player too, as his size suggests he should have been, and in retirement he will no doubt be a very good ambassador for the New Zealand meat company for whom he works. He is too far advanced to be a butcher but if ever the butcher should be absent ill, give him the knife and the carcass beware!

LANCE CAIRNS

THE BIOGRAPHY OF Phil Edmonds had a well and carefully chosen title. He was called a 'Singular Man'. He is indeed that: a charmer of strangers, an irritator of team-mates; a man who talks business in the dressing-room and cricket in the board-room; he has the apparently arrogant air of an ex-Colonial, yet he is more firmly anti-racist than many cricketers; he is a slow bowler who sometimes bowls bouncers; and a hard-hitting batsman who often blocks. In short, a contrary sort of character; but a character nonetheless, and a most talented cricketer too.

His mother was Belgian, so he is Phillippe Henri rather than Philip Henry. He spent his early boyhood in Zambia before returning to England to finish his education at Cranbrook and Cambridge. He was, I believe, an outstanding No. 8 Rugby forward: he certainly has the ideal solid build to thrive in a scrum, but it was cricket which quickly enabled him to become a public figure in his university days. His success as a left-arm spinner has always been based on a perfect action. He demonstrates admirably that cricket should be a 'sideways' game. Being Edmonds, of course, he conversely ignores the orthodox when batting, employing over the years an increasingly square stance. He has much talent as a batsman, indeed, but it has not always been used to best advantage. Nevertheless he can often be a cussed opponent.

He likes to give the appearance of being casual, often on the field, always off it, where he is a delightful companion unless you happen to be in the same dressing-room. Here, his love of an argument can cause tension.

Once he gets onto a cricket ground he is all bristling aggression. He talks a lot, claps his hands frequently to encourage the others and, when he himself is bowling well, can hardly bear the six-ball wait between overs lest his control over the opposing batsman, sometimes actual, sometimes imagined, be broken. Despite this confidence and belligerence he often seems to bowl within himself. He will vary his pace cleverly and mix the inswinging 'arm' ball with the leg-break, but what he sometimes fails to do is really to rip his fingers across the ball to produce the unplayable tweaker of which he is capable.

Perhaps he has not achieved everything he was capable of; but he has still been one of a mere handful of high-class spin bowlers in England for a long time, and if his start in Test cricket against Australia was a lucky one, nevertheless he should have played for England more than he did in his peak years. This may have owed something to the prejudice of one or two senior England players against him. The fault was theirs because although Edmonds may at times have been a difficult character, he has never had any malice in him. When they did have the courage to pick him on tours he proved an excellent ambassador, willing to talk to anyone from the groundsman to the most vicious of Fleet Street newshounds.

His wife, Frances, a bubbling extrovert, joined him on two tours and made herself at least as famous as her husband. This seemed to help Phil relax. It also suited the other England players, one of whom had previously been obliged to share a room with him and had found his habit of listening to BBC World Service bulletins in the middle of the night inconducive to sleep.

In 1987 Edmonds asked Middlesex if he could become a part-time player: an old-fashioned amateur. They gave him Sundays off to do some television work and catch up on various very successful business interests. It will be intriguing to see what he makes of life outside cricket. It is certain that he will find plenty to do, and talk about.

PHIL EDMONDS

IT SAYS MUCH FOR THE character of the tallest cricketer in Test history that he should have been a central figure in one of the most bitter disputes ever to have afflicted a county cricket club without anyone uttering a bitter word, or apparently even feeling a bitter thought, towards him personally.

Joel Garner himself might have felt some bitterness, for he had put down roots almost as long as himself (six feet eight inches) in Somerset, and even though by 1986 the spirit may have become more willing than the flesh, it was sad when the club decided towards the end of his benefit season to hand him his cards. He, with Ian Botham and Viv Richards, was one of the big three who had enabled Somerset to win trophies for the first time, but unlike the other two he had never given the impression that he had sometimes considered himself bigger than the game.

It was in the mid-1970s that we first got wind of a 'Big Bird' from Barbados. He first played for the West Indies in 1976–77, on the threshold of the World Series Cricket era. He not only took six wickets in his first Test, against Pakistan, but, going in at number eight, scored 43. Three Tests later he bagged a pair, and despite several useful contributions, his batting has not often fulfilled its potential, perhaps because crowds always expect him to hit the ball out of the ground, or at least to do something funny; or perhaps it was simply that he could never find a long enough bat. He plays with a normal-sized blade but an elongated handle. It still looks like a toy in the hands of a giant. When he really needs runs he often gets them: I saw him play very well indeed for his highest Test score of 60 in Brisbane. But as often as not, especially for the West Indies, he has settled for a policy of entertaining the customers.

The remarkable thing about his bowling is its accuracy and the balance and rhythm of his action. Few bowlers of any shape can match it. Garner is able to bowl fast and straight for long periods because he is not just a tall man but a big one in every respect, as he is frequently prepared to inform female admirers.

Seventeen stones of weight as well as at least eight feet of height from a high right arm go into every ball he bowls. It presents batsmen with a proposition which is at once frightening and perplexing. Their biggest problem is whether to go forward or back to good-length deliveries which, because of the steep angle from hand to pitch, are liable to bounce far higher than normal even on a mild pitch.

Garner is an intelligent bowler who reasons that if he can get a ball to rise awkwardly from a good length there is not much point, other than as a means of psychological warfare, in bowling bouncers. He would rather rap a batsman's knuckles than see him ducking beneath a flier.

He has been a prolific taker of wickets in all types of cricket with a Test record to be deeply proud of, and in One-Day Internationals for the West Indies and the big limited-overs tournaments in England he has frequently been a matchwinner, his devastating yorker spearing in on the middle and leg stumps to send scores of crestfallen batsmen back to the pavilion grateful only for the fact that their feet are still intact. When Barbados entrusted him with the captaincy he did the job impressively and in a characteristic mood of generosity gave away the prize-money to charity. He has considered social work as a career after cricket and has always had an interest in the underdog, unless he happens to be padded up at the other end of the pitch.

He is a typical Bajan off the field, with a broad smile and a hearty laugh, fond of beaches, girls and music. He brought some of the colour, sparkle and gaiety of Barbados to Taunton, and will take them wherever he travels.

JOEL GARNER

SMOOTH, MAN, SMOOTH. Michael Holding's bowling action was so smooth he could make you want to purr. He ran to the wicket as if on air, swift and silent as a fleeing antelope, head nodding and lolling like a new-born baby's. Never can so fast a bowler have had so soft a footfall. Umpires have found it rather unnerving not to be sure when he will arrive at the crease in a last-second swoosh past their left ear; batsmen have often been even more unnerved by the searing pace which results from that fluent glide towards the stumps.

That out-and-out pace enabled him once to take 13 wickets on a perfect batting pitch at The Oval – one on which Viv Richards and Dennis Amiss both scored double centuries. Never was it better demonstrated that the best bowlers will get wickets in any conditions. How unwise were the England team eight summers later to wish for, and generally to get, slow pitches rather than fast but true ones.

By 1984 Michael Holding was a different sort of bowler from the flat-out, straight-at-the-stumps express of 1976. Except for one memorable return to his long run in a spell, again at The Oval on a good wicket, which assured the West Indies of their total victory over England, he generally bowled well within his full pace, just occasionally letting it go, but otherwise approaching from a mere 18 yards or so after his thoughtful walk-back, kneading the ball like a cook working on the dough, concentrating on making it swing and, especially, cut off the seam.

He went over the top, in both senses, with short-pitched bowling less than most of his colleagues. More typical than his savage bombardment of the elderly Close and Edrich at Old Trafford in 1976 was his decision to bowl at only medium pace for Tasmania against England many years later on a dangerous pitch. Not that he would have taken the same decision in a Test match. He was a tough competitor, but to toughness were applied shrewdness and common sense. A sensitive, self-contained, thinking man, he speaks with the unmistakable slow, sing-song tones of the Jamaican. His smile lights a good-looking face. Cricketers and crowds alike have warmed to him, and he to them.

Perhaps this is why he has 'retired' from Test cricket more than once. Though he might have become an Olympic 400-metre hurdler rather than a professional cricketer, and although creaking muscles had forced him to make a definite decision to bid farewell to international cricket in 1987, he was still playing for Derbyshire a few months later, happy enough to parade before a few spectators beneath brooding clouds the talents which had thrilled packed thousands in stadia under the sun.

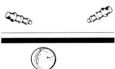

MICHAEL HOLDING

IF HE HAD BEEN created in fiction rather than fact Dennis Lillee would probably have sprung from the earth in the form of a dragon, spitting hell and breathing red flames of fury.

In the BBC's video archives there is a snatch of tape from the 1970–71 Ashes series. Illingworth's men are coming near to their decisive victory at Sydney and the young Lillee, cleaner-shaven and leaner than in his prime, has just cut the ball hard to slip, where he is caught at knee height in a perfectly straightforward way. But he refuses to walk! It needs an umpire's finger to confirm a dismissal obvious to everyone else on the ground. He moves reluctantly from his crease, scowling at all about him; by implication, if not by word itself, he has sworn to get even with his enemy. And time and again he was to do so.

Lillee's fight to regain fitness after the stress fractures in his back which threatened to end a fast-bowling career that had begun with devastating fury and brilliance, is a story of rare courage and determination. He sweated alone in the gym; strode out, equally alone, on long cross-country runs under the harsh, sapping sun of Western Australia. And he emerged as magnificent a physical specimen as has ever bowled fast for Australia, fuelled by what often seemed like a hot anger against batsmen, especially if they had the misfortune to be Poms.

Yet under the mop of hair, dark as night, beneath the brimstone face with its nose like a hawk's beak and eyes like burning coals, was a brain as cool and single-purposed as a snake waiting to envelop a lizard with a flick of its forked and poisoned tongue. This combination of motivation, physical strength and intelligence made him the supreme bowler of his era, at his retirement the most successful of all time and for most of his career the most feared, respected, lionized and reviled.

The man and the bowler were one and the same and cannot be separated. One will remember the bursts of theatrical fury; the petulant, spoiled-boy tantrums; but also the flashing smile and the desire always to please his audience, exemplified often when at the end of a wholehearted over he would accept the proferred autograph books over his shoulder at third-man and sign as many as possible of them between balls, handing them back to delighted owners with a smile and a quip. There was a certain logic, perhaps, in his unexpected production of his own autograph book from behind his back when he met The Queen in the official presentation during the Centenary Test at Melbourne. Officials may have been shocked, but Her Majesty was simply amused. Larrikin he may have been but, usually, a likeable one. He was never happier than when he was stirring the Establishment and throwing down challenges.

But he was at his best and most fulfilled when his mouth was shut and his body was talking. His action was a symphony, rolling melodiously through the long run-up to a glorious crescendo. The left arm swung towards the target as the heavy frame lifted from the ground and the right arm released the ball from its highest point before a power-packed descent and flowing follow-through. He could swing and cut the ball at will, and, whatever he may have said, in much publicized phrases, about bowling bouncers to hurt the batsmen, he did not, in fact, over-use that weapon as so many have done during and since his time. He bowled not to maim people, but to take their wicket in the shortest possible time.

DENNIS LILLEE

OF ALL THE GREAT fast bowlers of history Malcolm Marshall may well be the least spectacular. There is no surging run, no magnificent leap, no gilding of the lily for the public benefit. Like the modern motor-car Marshall is turbo-charged but economical.

He looks smaller than his five feet eleven inches and although he is muscular he is not what you would call a muscle-man. His approach to the wicket has neither the grace nor the brooding menace of some of his West Indian contemporaries. But not a step of it is wasted. For him there is no gradual acceleration, just a sharp stutter of the feet before he breaks into a direct sprint, smooth and swift.

When he delivers, the right arm comes over with unusual rapidity, having used a high left arm as a sighter. He has the deadly precision of a professional marksman. Most quick bowlers have a momentary jerk back of the body as they gather themselves for propulsion of the ball at maximum velocity. Marshall speeds past the stumps like a hundred-metre runner breasting the tape. It would not work for many bowlers but such is his superb athleticism and natural rhythm, he achieves red-hot pace, formidable accuracy and lethal movement off the seam.

Perhaps less merry than the average Bajan, Malcolm Marshall is nevertheless an easy-going character who was genuinely surprised to be chosen for his first tour for the West Indies after only a fleeting appearance for the island. Someone in the know had already appreciated the extraordinary pace he could develop. But it took him many years, against the hottest competition in world cricket, to establish his right to a regular place in the West Indies Test (and one-day) team. Having done so he gave no-one else a chance, taking over from Michael Holding as the quickest bowler and taking 20 and more wickets a series with a regularity quite alarming for his opponents.

Such success was not just the product of natural ability. He keeps himself superbly fit and never gives less than a hundred per cent for any team; he certainly does not stint himself for Hampshire where he has settled happily and bought a house. He has seen county cricket not just as a means of all-the-year-round employment but as a way to sharpen his skills both as a bowler and as a serious batsman with legitimate pretensions to being a genuine all-rounder at Test level. Like all West Indians he is stylish and he loves to hit the ball. He does not, as some fast bowlers do, worry about receiving a dose of his own medicine and when he broke a bone in the field against England at Leeds in 1984 he not only bowled better than ever but batted one-handed with cool courage.

He certainly tests the courage of those he bowls against. He has broken many a bone with a nasty, skidding bouncer which crunches into the body rather than sailing overhead. Such injuries give him no pleasure, but nor does he show much remorse. It is a tough game and Marshall obviously believes it should be played by tough men.

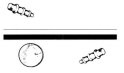

MALCOLM MARSHALL

BECAUSE SARFRAZ NAWAZ was an amiable eccentric, it was easy to overlook his quality as a fast-medium bowler. Strong as a carthorse, he would whip the ball either way off the seam at a lively pace by means of a good action wherein the left leg was classically braced, and if the moon was in the right quarter he could be dangerous to the best batsmen.

His most devastating spell of bowling was at Melbourne in 1978–79. He came on at a point when Australia needed only 77 to win in the fourth innings and took seven wickets for one run in 33 balls. He finished with nine wickets for 86 and would probably have had all ten had not Yallop, Australia's captain, been controversially run out. In the next match of a short but ill-tempered series, played at a time when world cricket was in turmoil, Sarfraz the hero became Sarfraz the villain. Following one run-out on each side, neither of them in the spirit of the game, he appealed successfully for an illegal handling of the ball by Australia's Andrew Hilditch, who had merely picked it up politely to hand it back to the bowler.

One would not normally think of Sarfraz as being an unsporting cricketer, far from it, but it was typical of him to do the unexpected or to go from one extreme to the other. He always went his own sweet way.

During another Test series, this time at home against England, he disappeared, for reasons never fully explained, after the first Test match of the series, although he was officially Pakistan's vice-captain. He turned up in, of all places, London, and told reporters he wanted to spend Christmas in England. Since he is a Moslem, this seemed a little odd! An affair of the heart, or, more likely perhaps, of the pocket in the prevailing atmosphere of general uncertainty in Pakistan cricket in the wake of the Packer affair, may have had something to do with his behaviour. Only in Pakistan could he have got away with it: a few weeks later he reappeared for the third Test, no doubt for a higher wage.

He had two separate spells as a county player for Northamptonshire and shared in their successes at Lord's in the 1976 Gillette Cup and 1980 Benson and Hedges Cup, when he took three for 23 in his 11 overs and many thought him the man of the match.

He could also be a very useful batsman and when a side underestimated him, as England did, for example, in 1974 at Leeds, he could turn a match with his fierce driving. He made 53 on that occasion, valuable runs in a low-scoring game, and then took seven wickets. On such a wicket where he would seam the ball about and make it bounce awkwardly, he was at his best.

He has got into political conflict since returning to Pakistan and giving up cricket, but those he played with will recall him with a smile for a game was seldom dull when Sarfraz was involved. He once bowled a succession of bouncers at Jeff Thomson, who thought it funny, and on another occasion at Joel Garner, who did not think it was funny. Sarfraz himself enjoyed both occasions.

SARFRAZ NAWAZ

ONLY THOSE WHO experienced it can understand quite what an impact Jeff Thomson made when he burst upon England in 1974. In the match before the Test at The Gabba he had played for Queensland, where he had moved after spending much of his youth on the beaches of New South Wales.

His first ball lifted from a length at electric speed to hit Dennis Amiss on the solar plexus. One could see Amiss's distinct shock. A shrewd gambler might in that instant have hurried to the nearest bookie and put his life-savings on Australia for the Ashes.

Thomson seemed to have come from nowhere, like one of those whirlwinds which sometimes blow up in Queensland, sucking up anything light in its powerful vortex. He had played one Test with, it was subsequently discovered, a broken foot. Not surprisingly he had not bowled at his best. He had subsequently lost his place in the New South Wales side but, coming in for the last match of the season, had bowled so fast that he had taken nine wickets and ruined Queensland's chances of winning the Sheffield Shield. Suitably impressed, Queensland invited him to play for them. More important, though, he had impressed Greg Chappell and other influential people. In Australia one really convincing performance gets round the grapevine quicker than in England. 'Forget his first Test match,' said the ones in the know, 'this Thomson is something special.'

Like some other very fast bowlers he was not at his peak for very long. But unlike some, Frank Tyson for example, he managed to remain fit and effective during a relatively long career – certainly long by Australian standards, despite one serious injury and various financial vicissitudes. The injury was to his powerful right shoulder, on which his action, with its violent swing of the body after an almost casual, far from graceful approach to the wicket, depended. It resulted from a collision with another player, Allan Turner, as both went for a high catch. Only very occasionally after his long-delayed return did he summon up the ferocious pace of 1974–76 when he and his great partner, Dennis Lillee, overwhelmed first England and then the West Indies.

That Thomson lasted so long was due in no small way to great determination allied to an easy-going nature. Various books written on his behalf have gone to town about his hatred of 'Poms'. It is difficult, in fact, to imagine him hating anyone. Neither an especially emotional nor a very intelligent man, he is the classic Australian outdoor boy, who has shown an aptitude for gardening and made a successful career in advising others on garden layout since his retirement from cricket. He failed despite immense efforts to help Queensland to a Sheffield Shield title, but on his last tour of England he reached 200 Test wickets, a just reward for an honest, wholehearted bowler who never gave less than his best.

JEFF THOMSON

FIRST CAUGHT SIGHT of Bob Willis from about 40 yards during a club match in Surrey. He seemed to be all arms and legs, topped by a narrow, lugubrious face and a mop of brown hair. For a teenager he was surprisingly fast and he soon had me caught at first slip cutting, the first slip standing for him where third-man normally stood for club opening bowlers.

Two winters after this Willis was flown out as a replacement for Alan Ward in Illingworth's side in Australia. He had the time of his life and shared valuably in the team's success. Twelve years later he had the signal honour of leading England in Australia himself. He performed the job with pride and intense determination, bowling superbly.

He was never, however, a natural leader of men. On the contrary he always went his own way and never managed to communicate very effectively with any but his closest friends. Something secret and intense seemed always to be ticking over behind staring eyes and a bland expression. A deep, monotone voice combined with this to give many people the idea that there might be a vacant brain underneath the mop. In fact, there was a mind which thought a good deal and knew what it wanted.

In the mood – and for England, at least, he always was – he could be a devilish opponent, running in at full bore with heavy tread from a long way and hurling the ball at the batsman, or his stumps, with all his might. Being chest-on in delivery he was never a great swinger of the ball but he could always get nasty bounce and very often movement either way off the seam. If he were never an artist in this respect, tending to thump it down on the seam and wait to see what happened, he nevertheless had much shrewdness in finding out a batsman's weakness and then probing it with precise accuracy. He spared no-one a bouncer if he thought it would get them out more quickly and he was able to keep going through sheer will-power when feet which often bled as well as ached were protesting bitterly. Getting Bob Willis the right boots was a problem on all his many overseas tours.

His career had two watersheds. After the unexpected call to Australia he asked Surrey for the county cap which would have guaranteed his future at The Oval. His demand refused, he moved to Warwickshire, who treated him with great understanding throughout a career in which he seldom gave them the same unstinting service he rendered to England. His second Rubicon was crossed in 1976 when the West Indies were first deploying four fast bowlers. Tony Greig, then England captain, told Willis that he needed to be much fitter if he wished to give them their own medicine consistently. He set out to prepare himself more suitably by going for long cross-country runs.

His most memorable piece of bowling was in the second innings at Headingley in 1981 when England won after following on, an achievement with only one precedent. He took eight for 43, bowling flat out down the hill and achieving ferocious pace and bounce. He looked like a man possessed, wild-eyed and expressionless, locked inside a cocoon of concentration and determination.

He will be more relaxed, no doubt, now that he is retired and has turned for a living to talking about the game to which he has always had such an intense and devoted attraction. He has always had a slightly zany sense of humour and now that he has settled down with a wife and children he will no longer be tormented through long sleepless nights, worrying about the frailties of the England batting or the strength of the opposition's. Nor will he need so much recourse to the hypnotic tapes prepared for him by an Australian psychologist to make his approach more positive. How he worked and worried for all those wickets!

BOB WILLIS

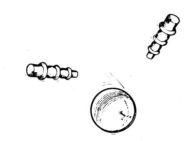

UMPIRES AND COMMENTATORS

JOHN ARLOTT IS UNIQUE. When one thinks of him one thinks first of a voice. But that voice would never have become famous had not its owner possessed an unusual depth of humanity and a rare breadth of knowledge about cricket and much else besides.

It was his intellect, combined with a rare capacity for compassion and a wonderfully observant eye which made him a cricket commentator of unrivalled range. With his sharp memory for cricket history he could relate anything taking place on the field in front of him to something which had happened before, placing it judiciously in context. What is more he could describe it with an effortless recourse to a wide vocabulary and a poet's sense of drama and colour.

Add to these qualities a sense of humour and a mellow voice with a gentle Hampshire accent that engaged many and offended no-one and it is easy to understand John Arlott's fame as a cricket commentator. He could not be directly replaced nor precisely emulated. Like all true originals he was inimitable – yet perhaps only a handful of high-ranking politicians have been more frequently imitated by a host of amateur impressionists.

Since the advent of television, 'stars' have been two a penny. Most, however, are ephemeral. Radio helped John Arlott achieve a lasting fame, the size and substance of which none of us can have appreciated until his retirement in 1980. Every last appearance at a cricket ground was marked by a wave of public affection towards him. Off the field poor John, the great connoisseur of food and wine, was overwhelmed by hospitality. Everyone wanted to give him a good send-off.

Although he was as ambitious and acquisitive as the next man, he never really sought fame. He wanted to mix with friends, not celebrities. He was happiest with a small company drinking wine at his own dinner table in Hampshire.

Life has remained, since his retirement, just as convivial at the Arlott table in Alderney. In the BBC commentary box we have missed his knowledge, the shaggy-dog stories he told off-mike with such relish, his ability to induce gifts of champagne or vintage wine and his peerless quality as a professional who took as much trouble over the small tasks as he did with the big ones.

John had a quite prodigious appetite for wine, yet only once did I see it get the better of him, and then only because he was taking some pills recommended by his doctor. He and Fred Trueman were summing up the morning's play in the lunch interval. Fred concluded a lengthy dissertation by saying: 'That's what I think anyway, John, I don't know if you'd agree . . .' He turned to see John slumped forward fast asleep beside him. 'Well,' said Fred, with admirable aplomb, 'John's nodding his head in assent but the lunch interval is pressing on so I think it's time I handed you back to the studio. From Lord's for the time being, goodbye.'

Rather than dulling the senses, wine seemed often to sharpen John Arlott's wit. Sometimes, late at night in a hotel amidst a Test match, it would loosen his tongue and dredge up characteristics which he often kept hidden. At such times he would get deeply emotional. He is, indeed, a passionate man, but at the microphone or typewriter, the brain was always in control.

JOHN ARLOTT

THE TELEVISION commentator, whose face and voice are known to millions in Australia and many millions more in Britain, is *really* known to very few; perhaps only to his wife, Daphne, who became known to Richie through being the most efficient secretary that the formidable E. W. Swanton ever had.

Richie is pretty formidable too, in his own quiet way. He keeps his own counsel. He does a high-pressure job at a savage pace all the year round literally without blinking an eyelid. Never was a more impassive face, a glassier, more unyielding countenance displayed before a camera. But from lips which barely seem to move, in accents and phrases all his own, come, year after year, match after match, words of pungent authority. His knowledge and his impartiality stand out as strongly as his determination to present cricket and its players in the best possible light. Whatever he may have taken out of the game, he has undoubtedly been good for it. No-one else has found such favour with the vast majority of cricket viewers at both ends of the world for so long.

That cool exterior is no mask. Behind it lies a calculating brain and a sharp wit. His organization and self-discipline are as immaculate as his attire. Never a crooked tie; never a hair out of place; never hurried; never late; never ruffled. At the end of a day's commentary he introduces the highlights. The editing of these may sometimes be well, sometimes badly balanced. But the man who introduces them is seldom anything other than shrewd in his appraisal of the events of the day or the position of the match. Not that the highlights mark the end of his day. He still has his column to attend to, and often more stories than just one to write. He drives himself extraordinarily hard.

He was the same as a player, and especially as a captain. Such fastidiousness might have made him a rather dull, utilitarian cricketer. He was actually a bold, attacking one: a daring, handsome batsman; an athletic fielder who at Lord's in 1956 held a catch from the blade of Cowdrey's bat in the gully which knocked him over and took the breath away from everyone who saw it; and a leg-break bowler with a perfect action. It gained him more Test wickets than any other leg-spinner in history.

But it was for his captaincy that he became most honoured. How could England have failed to beat Australia in 1958–59 with a side which included May, Cowdrey, Bailey, Dexter, Evans, Graveney, Laker, Lock, Loader, Tyson, Statham and Trueman? Well, one of many reasons, by all accounts, was that Benaud out-captained May. He was quick to see a gap and to go for it; shrewd in finding the right bowlers for the conditions; adept at intimidating the opposition with hustling fields and aggressive bowling. He had been on losing sides against England in 1954–55 and 1956, and he had every motivation for revenge.

In 1961, with Ted Dexter now his adversary, he famously stole a match which Dexter seemed to have won for England by a marvellous attacking innings. Knowing it was hit or miss, Benaud began bowling round the wicket into the rough and, making light of a damaged right shoulder, he spun England to an embarrassing defeat.

Benaud the opportunist and the competitor. He has shown the same quick-witted eye for the main chance in his working life and maintained an admirable standard. He relaxes by playing golf, approaching the game with the same meticulous care he applies to everything else. His clubs are the best you can find; his swing has a professional's arc and strength. He likes to win, and usually does.

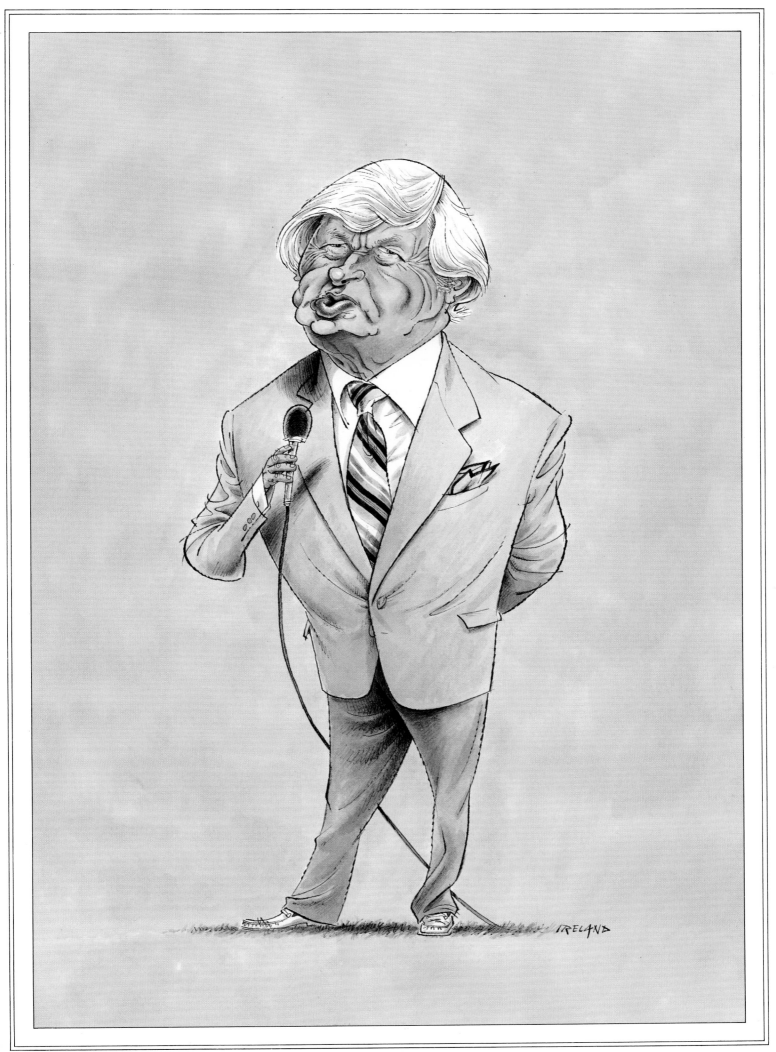

RICHIE BENAUD

HAROLD BIRD WAS a brilliant cricketer as a young man. You have to be to become a county cricketer. But when players reach that exalted level, the going gets really tough. H.D. Bird played 14 matches for Yorkshire and once scored 181 not out against Glamorgan at Bradford. 'But Yorkshire were that strong I lost me place in t'next game.'

He moved to Leicestershire and played for them for the first five seasons of the Sixties. In 1960 he scored more than 1,000 runs. Yet only the devotees would have heard of him these days if he had not decided to try his hand at umpiring. The obscure county cricketer has become the most famous umpire in England since Frank Chester and, internationally, the best known there has ever been. Television, and his own excellence, have made him a star.

Nowadays he signs his letters: 'Dicky Bird, Test umpire.' The two are synonymous. A bachelor from Barnsley, he is married to cricket and loves it more passionately than the dearest wife. He is a man on top of his job, quick-witted, sharp-eyed and not just well-versed in the game's laws but positively bathed in them, so that knowledge and wisdom of its subtleties will ooze out of him as from a sponge. Yet he frets and struts on the stage, and off it he worries like a harassed schoolboy over a difficult maths prep.

'Did I do right, David?' he will ask of his colleague as soon as they reach the sanctuary of the umpires' room. 'It would have 'it middle-stump, I'm not bothered about that, but did it pitch in line, David?'

Before there is time for a reply he will answer his own question. 'I think he were out, David. I think he put pad outside line after it had 'it 'im. I think it pitched in line and would have 'it middle stump. I think he were out, David. I do. I think he were out. . . .'

Over a pint, or more often an orange juice, he will start to unwind, talking in a voice which becomes louder the greater the number of people he is addressing, about incidents in the day's play, exciting new batsmen he has seen, bowlers who move the ball yards, spinners who give it a real tweak, wicket-keepers as quick as lime. He is generous in his opinions, too. Ask him who the best 'keeper in England is and he will say: 'Bruce French', with a decisive thrust of the jaw. 'Frenchie? Brilliant 'keeper, Chris.' Then you may mention what Jack Richards did in Australia and he will add: 'Bruce French or Jack Richards. Nothing to choose between them, Chris. Nothing to choose between French, Richards or young Steve Rhodes. Brilliant 'keeper, Rhodes, Chris.'

'What about Jack Russell of Gloucestershire?' one asks, innocently.

'Best in the country, Chris. Best of the lot.'

Thus would he go on in circles, cheerfully, all night, as long as the talk is cricket. He has some marvellous stories, about men he played with, umpires he has stood with, and his own eccentric exploits, starting with the time that a policeman apprehended him as he was clambering over the fence at The Oval at crack of dawn in his anxiety to be there in plenty of time for his first game.

'What do you think you are doing up there, young man?'

'I am officiating in a cricket match, officer.'

'At five-thirty in the morning, sir?'

'An umpire must always be prepared, officer.'

 And Dicky always is.

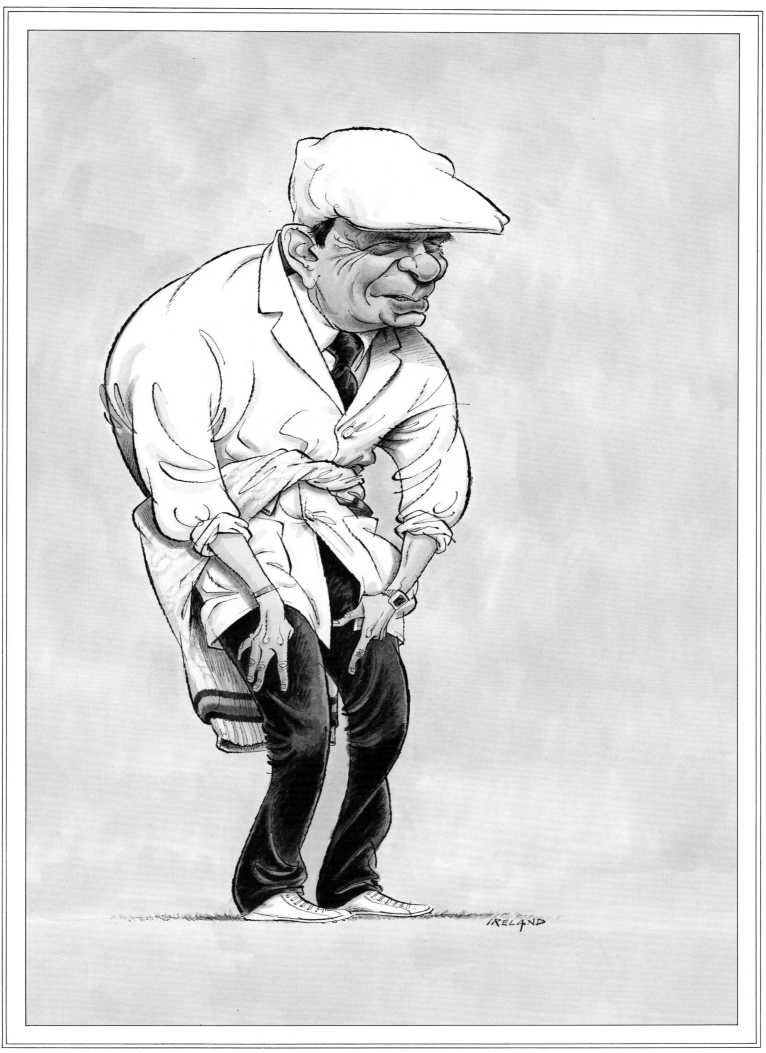

'DICKY' BIRD

LIKE OL' MAN RIVER, the irrepressible B.J. rolls into the commentary box every spring, fresh as a primrose and bright as the willows in their early-season green. The game would not be the same without him and to me, often coming back from a wearying tour, his cheery return to the BBC box is an annual tonic. I am sure it is the same for the listeners.

Brian bubbles with enthusiasm, both for cricket and for life. He is frequently a source of interesting gossip about cricketing friends and although at his age he could be forgiven for being a little out of touch with some aspects of the modern game, he is, in fact, always on the ball, up to date with any changes in the regulations (especially the tea regulations) and well informed about promising players.

He remains very much on the ball in his commentaries too. His listeners get a bonus every time: not just the passage of each ball bowled, but a hundred and one additional titbits, which add spice to the main meal. The vast majority of his listeners appreciate the quick-witted puns and the ready recourse to a deep fund of cricketing stories and it is mainly to Brian that *Test Match Special* owes its reputation for friendliness and fun. Like Cleopatra, 'age cannot wither him nor custom stale his infinite variety'.

'Infinite variety' may, actually, be stretching a point, although there is almost no statement that B.J. cannot turn into a pun, and no situation, cricketing or otherwise, in which he cannot find some humour. To criticize Brian, as some have done, for excessive levity or frivolity is unfair. If all the fun and light-heartedness which he brings to his commentaries, greatly to the enjoyment of most of his listeners, were at the expense of telling the story of the game in progress, the criticism would be merited. But it is not. Listeners can rely on a fair and accurate description of the match as well as an entertaining one.

No-one loves cricket more than Brian Johnston and few know the game better or do more to enhance its good name. Seventy-five in June 1987, he seemed then about as likely to retire as Mrs Thatcher. When he eventually does, his marvellous sense of fun and peerless gift of the gab will be missed both by his colleagues in the box and his listeners.

BRIAN JOHNSTON

IT IS NEVER EASY to be an umpire; it is harder still to be a Test umpire; and it is hardest of all to be a Test umpire in India where the scrutiny of the crowds is more intense than anywhere else and where the perpetrator of a mistake will be laughed to scorn – or, worse, threatened with serious violence.

For many years Swaroop Kishen was one of the best umpires in India and he was not only respected by the players but loved by the crowds. His very appearance made him a character. He was so fat that people said his white coat made a sight-screen unnecessary. He chewed betel nuts to aid his concentration and he sweated profusely under the hot Indian sun. One or two cricketers preferred to stay upwind of him; but they liked him for his geniality, his honesty, his unflappability and his accuracy, until his last series when, like many good umpires before him (notably Australia's Mel McInnes) he lost his grip.

Given the tensions of having to make hairline decisions which could have a crucial bearing on matches involving a great deal of money and prestige, not to mention the livelihoods of individual players, it is hardly surprising that occasionally an umpire's judgment should fail him.

Swaroop in Hindi means 'sweet of face or feature'. In the words of the song he must have been a beautiful baby. There was certainly, too, a sweetness in the smile, slightly sad, which highlighted his podgy features when the day's cricket was done and the fever of battle over.

He comes from Srinigar, the cool northern city of Kashmir. He worked for many years in the auditing department of a Government Service in Delhi. Of Bhramin stock, he used to bat at number three in his youth but umpired his first match at the age of only 18. It took him a long time to reach the top, for he did not stand in a Test until he was 48, in 1978.

Once there, he quickly established himself, mainly because of his excellent umpiring, but partly because of his high public profile. He was invited to officiate in a tournament in Sharjah in the Middle East and told Dicky Bird as they walked out together that a long-held ambition of his had been fulfilled. It showed a touching affection for the game which made him, for a few years at least, more famous than many a talented player.

SWAROOP KISHEN

ACKNOWLEDGMENT

The Publishers would like
to thank Adrian Murrell/All-Sport
for their help in providing photographic references
to assist John Ireland in the
development of his caricatures.